Concise guides
to planning

Green Infrastructure Planning

Green Infrastructure Planning

Reintegrating Landscape in Urban Planning

Ian Mell

First published in 2019 by Lund Humphries

Lund Humphries
Office 3, Book House
261A City Road
London EC1V 1JX
UK
www.lundhumphries.com
Green Infrastructure Planning
© Ian Mell, 2019
All rights reserved

ISBN (hardback): 978-1-84822-275-5
ISBN (eBook PDF): 978-1-84822-287-8
ISBN (eBook ePub): 978-1-84822-302-8
ISBN (eBook ePub Mobi): 978-1-84822-303-5

Concise Guides to Planning (Print): ISSN 2516-8177
Concise Guides to Planning (Online): ISSN 2516-8185

A Cataloguing-in-Publication record for this book is
available from the British Library.

Designed by Stefi Orazi Studio
Cover illustration by Stefi Orazi
Set in Favorit

Images © Ian Mell, p. 32 © Puravankara

Dedication
For Theofila and Francisco — this hopefully explains
why we talk about trees and grass and spend so much
time in parks.

Contents

Foreword

This excellent book provides a unique introduction to green infrastructure, taking the reader through the basics of what it is and grappling with some of the intricacies of putting ideas into practice. One of the great strengths of the book is that it is a joy to read, helped by the copious use of well-illustrated case study material drawn from around the world, in particular China, France, Germany, India, the UK and USA.

I took home three key messages from this book, though I know there could have been many more. First, that green infrastructure is as much about people as it is about nature, particularly in cities. This is linked to the idea of multi-functionality: that we should be looking to create green infrastructure that can deliver environmental, social and economic advantages. The second message is that there is a fast-growing repertoire of tools that can be drawn upon, but which ones will work best in any particular area will depend on an area's existing landscape characteristics and what the people of the area want to do to improve it. Thirdly, that successful development of green infrastructure is a creative process that involves planners working together with environmentalists, scientists, engineers, developers and local communities, building up support and attracting investment by producing evidence of the multiple positive impacts that green infrastructure can generate – from better health, to improving biodiversity and ecosystems, through to providing real estate value uplift.

Green infrastructure planning is more than anything a call to be imaginative in how to think about a better future world – and who wouldn't want to be at the forefront of work that can achieve that. This book provides multiple inspiring examples of the benefits of working to improve green infrastructure in diverse situations around the world, along with salutary advice about difficulties that can sometimes be encountered along the way.

Graham Haughton, Series Editor

Preface

Green infrastructure planning has come a long way in a relatively short period of time. It has developed from a partial, specialist and limited approach to landscape resource assessment into a form of landscape planning that is increasingly used globally to meet a range of social, economic and ecological needs. Green infrastructure is not a panacea for urban and societal ills. Alternatively, it sets out a range of options that planners, architects, landscape specialists, engineers and the public can use to make their homes, neighbourhoods and cities more sustainable.

However, how we facilitate this process is not straightforward. We have had to provide evidence of what benefits, be they social, ecological or economic, green infrastructure can provide to a range of stakeholders. Furthermore, we are yet to convince the public and the business community of the added value that green infrastructure can provide. Although we have seen several key advocates in the UK and further afield promote the use of green infrastructure – including the Town and Country Planning Association (TCPA) and Natural England in the UK, the Conservation Fund in the USA and Institut für Landes- und Stadtentwicklungsforschung (ILS) in Germany – there is also a certain amount of scepticism from the development sector and within government in some countries regarding the value of green infrastructure in practice, which will be discussed. We therefore see an enduring question within green infrastructure discussions asking how we reinforce the positives of investing in landscape resources, especially at a time when finances are becoming increasingly limited.

The following text aims to introduce these discussions outlining the ways in which green infrastructure planning can enable planners, landscape architects, engineers and environmentalists to understand how we can use landscape principles to deliver more sustainable urban planning. The book discusses the rise of green infrastructure as a concept, outlining its main principles: ecological and landscape connectivity, access to nature, promoting human-environmental interactions and valuation of the landscape and an understanding of the multi-functional nature of green and blue space highlighting the added value of investing in landscapes at a number of scales and in a number of ways.

To ensure clarity in these discussions the book uses key questions to provide a foundation to its explorations. These include: what is green infrastructure? Why should we develop it? Who uses it? What socio-economic and ecological value does it provide? Each of these questions will be debated to guide practitioners in their exploration of how green infrastructure can be used, in what situations it will thrive and what mistakes can be avoided.

Using multiple examples from practice in the UK, Europe, North America and Asia the book illustrates how good policy ideas, innovative practice and committed advocates can help develop more sustainable and ecologically focussed urban landscapes. It also examines the complexities faced by decision-makers and practitioners who are aiming to ensure that green infrastructure is considered alongside other built infrastructure resources.

The book will be of interest to practitioners, policy-makers and environmental groups as it illustrates how different approaches to green infrastructure investment can deliver different, yet innovative urban landscapes. In an era where the political and financial support for landscape planning is under threat the book proposes a set of design, delivery and management options that can be used to create 'win-win' situations for green infrastructure investment.

Acknowledgements

I would like to thank a number of people for their assistance in making this publication and others possible.

First, I would like to thank Maggie Roe, as always, for her support and guidance. Second, I would like to thank Clive Davies, Dave Shaw, Juliet Staples and John Henneberry for providing me with opportunities to explore green infrastructure in the UK and Europe. In addition, I would like to express my thanks to Jack Ahern in Amherst, Sejal Patel and Saswat Bandyopadhyay in Ahmedabad, Bing Cheng in Suzhou and Karsten Rusche, Mario Reimer and Jost Wilker in the Ruhr. Third, I would like to thank all the students and staff who let me discuss, examine and test my green infrastructure ideas on them, many of whom have become or are going on to be great planners and landscape professionals. Fourth, I would like to thank John Sturzaker who has been listening to discussions of trees and grass for over a decade, as well as that joke. Finally, I would like to thank Alice, because she makes all this possible, and Thea and Francisco: someday this will make our holidays make sense.

I would also like to express my gratitude to Graham Haughton, the Editor of this series, Val Rose for her help with the project and the other members of the Lund Humphries team.

Chapter 1

Introduction: Why Do We Need Green Infrastructure?

Green infrastructure encompasses many different spaces and activities. It includes where we take our children to play on a Sunday afternoon, the spaces where we see ducks and squirrels when living in the city, and the areas in which many seek peace, quiet or relaxation after a busy week. For my part, these activities all take place in Heaton Park in north Manchester; this location provides recreational and leisure activities and access to 642 acres of nature in an urban setting. It is also less than five minutes' walk from my house. All of these factors are key principles when discussing green infrastructure.

Heaton Park is used to highlight the multiple benefits of green infrastructure, and to illustrate that it can be something very simple: a park. It can also be something more complicated, a reconstructed wetland for example, as the following chapters will explore. Thus, when we talk about 'green infrastructure' this book argues it is something we are all inherently familiar with, although we might not give it much thought or use that terminology.

Any discussion of green infrastructure therefore starts with the question: what does it constitute? This depends on who you are and where you are from. In my experience it comprises trees, green spaces, waterways, rivers and lakes, meadows and woodlands that are part of our urban areas. However, it is also the forests, moorlands, river systems and coastlines that populate our wider landscapes. In addition to these natural spaces, green infrastructure can be thought of as the man-made, i.e. managed parklands, formal gardens, allotments, canal paths, and the green walls and roofs that we see increasingly across our cities. Thus, green infrastructure is the wide range of green, blue and open spaces that we interact with in our urban, urban-fringe and rural landscapes. Due to such variability, green infrastructure can be thought of as a jack-of-all-trades term in landscape and urban planning, as it encompasses the spaces that are, at the most basic level, not made of concrete or bricks. Moreover, how we interact with and experience these various green spaces is key to how we value and plan for the landscapes around us.

At its heart, green infrastructure constitutes the places, the elements, the experiences and feelings, and the benefits that we derive from the physical landscape around us. This does not mean we disregard aspects of the built infrastructure, i.e. grey infrastructure such as roads or buildings, but focus more directly on the ecological resources, which we see around us. Consequently, it has proven difficult to arrive at a definitive record of what aspects of the environment can be considered as green infrastructure, although Natural England provided a thorough list in their 2009 guidance. This is both an asset and a drawback. It allows those interested in 'landscape' to draw on a range of examples to promote the development of green infrastructure. Those less sold on its value, however, point to a lack of clarity about what green infrastructure is and how it should be used. To address this, there is a growing evidence base supporting investment in green infrastructure as an approach to landscape and urban management within planning, among architectural and landscape professionals and even in community discussions.

This book sets out to explain what green infrastructure is, how we should be using or investing in it, what problems there are with this process, and how we can use the knowledge to create better places to live, work and recreate using green infrastructure. This is a complex process, and indeed one that requires an understanding of the various political, economic, socio-cultural and ecological factors that influence development. Whilst this text does not assume it can or will provide the solution to how best to 'do' green infrastructure, it will set out why we should, how we can and what benefits it can provide. It draws on over a decade of experience researching, teaching and implementing green infrastructure projects in the UK, Europe, North America and Asia, and a corresponding engagement with the policy, practice, design and financial aspects of landscape enhancement.

Providing the foundations for this discussion, this chapter sets out where the ideas of green infrastructure planning have developed from, and shows how greenways, landscape ecology, sustainable communities and, more recently, ecosystem services and Nature-Based Solutions (NBS) have influenced its use. It introduces the key principles of green infrastructure, namely: connectivity, access to nature, human-environmental interactions, the value of nature and multi-functionality. It goes on to link these principles to the disciplines that work with the concept: planning, architecture, landscape, ecology, engineering, environmental management and sustainable place-making advocates. The chapter concludes by outlining the key themes of scale, the scope of investment and how different people use green infrastructure in policy and practice, which structure the discussions in subsequent chapters.

Chapter 2 debates the ways in which green infrastructure is linked to the physical layout of our landscapes and how connectivity with, and between, people and nature is beneficial to society, the economy and the environment. This discussion looks at how different approaches to investment in green infrastructure leads to the design of landscapes that offer multiple benefits simultaneously. Chapter 3 extends this debate focussing on how people interact with and perceive the landscapes around them. This includes a discussion of how different socio-cultural and ecological factors influence interactions with the environment, and asks whether it also limits the value people place on green infrastructure at a local, city and wider scale. Chapter 4 reflects on a fundamental question for many green infrastructure advocates: what does it look like? This outlines the various interpretations of green infrastructure by different stakeholders highlighting how the diversity of investment in landscape planning addresses localised and societal needs and aspirations. The following section, Chapter 5, discusses the scale at which green infrastructure is delivered to explain how bigger, bolder and more innovative interventions in urban greening can be beneficial to our cities. This focusses on the role regeneration, the management of water resources and the ways in which ecological systems can be managed to promote sustainability. Chapter 6 utilises the examples presented in Chapters 1–5 to debate how current policy, guidance and practice influence the development of green infrastructure. This chapter reflects on the variety of advocates coming from planning, landscape, development and community groups supporting green infrastructure, and how this is affecting delivery. The final chapter draws on the content of the previous chapters and outlines a set of policy, practice and financing proposals for those interested in working with green infrastructure. These are key to avoid the mistakes of previous investment and to promote inclusive, innovative and evidenced approaches to landscape management. This final chapter also asks what and where next for green infrastructure, and importantly how we get there.

To contextualise this discussion, it is both necessary and informative to reflect on what green infrastructure is, where the concept has developed from, how we use it, and what benefits it provides for people, society and the environment.

What is green infrastructure?

When discussing green infrastructure, it is important to remember that our understanding of it is shaped by the socio-economic, ecological and political context in which we work. Thus, there is a corresponding need to understand how differences in geography and time influence interpretations of green infrastructure. Consequently, when debating what green infrastructure is we must remember to think about the location we are investing in, what is there already, what difference the project will make to the existing landscape and how an investment in landscape changes over time.

At the centre of this debate is an understanding of what green infrastructure is. This means both conceptually in terms of definitions, as shown in Table 1, and also physically, in the types of spaces and investments that can be considered as 'green infrastructure'. The latter is significant to organisations looking to invest in urban greening and landscape improvements, as they need to know what they are investing in and what it will look like; something that landscape architects do well and planners maybe less so!

To date, several definitions have been offered outlining what various academics and planning institutions consider green infrastructure to be. A selection is listed in Table 1 for comparison highlighting how they differ in scope, brevity and in the types of landscapes proposed as 'green infrastructure'. Although these vary in scale and socio-economic and ecological value, they do show a comparability in terms of the key principles and landscape resources they use. Understanding the differences in the way that people view green infrastructure is a good starting point to increase our awareness of how it should be used. It also helps to move beyond the simplistic view of green infrastructure as being grass, gardens and trees, as different definitions allow us to focus on the variation in ecological, social and economic benefits that green space can provide.

Table 1
Green infrastructure definitions

Source	Definition
Benedict and McMahon (2006) *Green Infrastructure: Linking Landscapes and Communities*	'Green infrastructure is an interconnected network of green spaces that conserves natural ecosystems, values and functions and provides associated benefits to human populations. Green infrastructure is the ecological framework needed for environmental, social and economic sustainability.'
Williamson (2003) *Growing with Green Infrastructure*	'Our nation's natural life support system – an interconnected network of protected land and water that supports native species, maintains natural ecological processes, sustains air and water resources and contributes to the health and quality of life for America's communities and people.'

Town and Country Planning Association (2004) *Biodiversity by Design – Projects and Publications*	'Green infrastructure is a sub-regional network of protected sites, nature reserves, green spaces and greenway linkages. Green infrastructure should provide for multi-functional uses i.e. wildlife, recreational and cultural experience, as well as delivering ecological services, such as flood protection and microclimate control. It should operate at all spatial scales from urban centres through to open countryside.'
TEP (2005) *Advancing the Delivery of Green Infrastructure: Targeting Issues in England's Northwest*	'Green infrastructure: the physical environment within and between cities, towns and villages. The network of open spaces, waterways, gardens, woodlands, green corridors, street trees and open countryside that brings many social, economic and environmental benefits to local people and communities.'
Natural England and Landuse Consultants (2009) *Green Infrastructure Guidance*	'Green infrastructure is a strategically planned and delivered network comprising the broadest range of high quality green spaces and other environmental features. It should be designed and managed as a multi-functional resource capable of delivering those ecological services and quality of life benefits required by the communities it serves and needed to underpin sustainability. Its design and management should also respect and enhance the character and distinctiveness of an area with regard to habitats and landscape types. Green infrastructure includes established green spaces and new sites and should thread through and surround the built environment and connect the urban area to its wider rural hinterland. Consequently it needs to be delivered at all spatial scales from sub-regional to local neighbourhood levels, accommodating both accessible natural green spaces within local communities and often much larger sites in the urban fringe and wider countryside.'

Mell (2010) *Green Infrastructure: Concepts, Perceptions and Its Use in Spatial Planning*	'Green infrastructure are the resilient landscapes that support ecological, economic and human interests by maintaining the integrity of, and promoting landscape connectivity, whilst enhancing the quality of life, place and the environment across different landscape boundaries.'
Landscape Institute (2013) *Green Infrastructure: An Integrated Approach to Land Use*	'GI is the network of natural and semi-natural features, green spaces, rivers and lakes that intersperse and connect villages, towns and cities. Individually, these elements are GI assets, and the roles that these assets play are GI functions. When appropriately planned, designed and managed, the assets and functions have the potential to deliver a wide range of benefits – from providing sustainable transport links to mitigating and adapting the effects of climate change.'

Variation of the type shown in Table 1 suggests that our understanding of what green infrastructure is has changed over time, and is being influenced by the growing evidence base of research, policies, guidance notes and projects that are supporting the use of the concept. What we also see is a focussing of understanding around a discrete number of principles, thematic areas and types of landscape features that are being considered as green infrastructure in mainstream planning. These appear to transcend geographical and disciplinary boundaries and help to generate buy-in from different organisations for green infrastructure. Moreover, the key principles outlined in the green infrastructure literature are, as noted above: connectivity, access to nature, the development of an integrated form of landscape and urban planning, a multi-disciplinary approach to management, a growing awareness of the multi-scalar benefits of investment in landscape, and finally the establishment of multi-functional social, ecological and economic benefits from a green infrastructure resource. Each of these principles can, and should, be considered in any discussion of green infrastructure planning. What is interesting about these principles is their connectedness as a set of unifying ideas that support a design, investment and management of our landscapes, which are discussed below.

An example of each of these principles is Central Park, New York. Central Park is located close to residential neighbourhoods, commercial property and tourist attractions. It is serviced by several subway stations and public footpaths, and offers a variety of landscape types and features that allow people to interact with the park in different ways simultaneously. The park is managed by the Central Park Conservancy, which oversees its current funding and longer-term development. The Conservancy works with the City of New York to ensure that the park's atmospheric and flood mitigation benefits are linked to the city's wider climate change strategy. The park is also able to accommodate thousands of people at once participating in a variety of activities, thus making the site socially and economically multi-functional. The success of Central Park as a multi-functional green space reflects its accessible central Manhattan location, its size, its variable landscape and its promotion of the most attractive and interactive site in New York.

As with Central Park we can identify the following principles as supporting effective green infrastructure development in other locations. First, connectivity is a key issue, as it reflects the ways in which elements of the urban, urban-fringe and rural landscapes are connected. The Public Rights of Way network in the UK is one example of this principle in action. Connectivity can be achieved through the development of physical spaces such as parks, greenways and river corridors that link people with the environments around them. It can also be created through effective literal, digital and metaphorical signposting of green spaces to ensure people are aware of and able to interact with their environments. Additional biodiversity benefits can also be derived from connective urban environments including the creation and maintenance of habitat mosaics, such as Wicken Fen and the Great Fen projects in the east of England, which allow different species to move around an environment successfully. Such spaces are important in supporting ecological diversity and colonisation of new areas. Moths, birds and amphibians are just some of the species that find connective green infrastructure invaluable in their search for suitable habitats. In the USA, the development of greenways in Boston and St Louis has been a key component in the increase in biodiverse urban habitats.

Aligned with the creation of connective landscape features, green infrastructure also promotes access to nature. This is a key component of forging human-environmental relationships, which is particularly vital for children, where exposure to nature has been shown to facilitate a lifelong engagement with landscape resources. The promotion of Forest Schools by the Mersey Forest in north-west England and the Natural Health Service programme by the UK's National Health Service (NHS) highlight the long-term health benefits of interaction with the landscape in helping to address asthma, obesity, cardiovascular disease and mental health issues, and an increased pace of recovery from ill health or injury in hospital patients in the USA. Moreover, accessible green spaces in and around urban areas have been shown to improve educational attainment in children in Scandinavia and Japan.

How we access nature is not simply driven by proximity, but also by the quality and functionality of a green space, as seen in the Central Park example. We can argue that green infrastructure which is accessible by foot, bicycle or public transport and which provides a variety of opportunities to engage with nature is viewed as being more valuable than mono-functional landscape. We can therefore ask which is more interesting, an urban woodland, a wildflower meadow or a large area of grass, when we look to invest in green infrastructure.

There is also a corresponding need to ensure that knowledge of these principles is embedded within a wider discussion of planning policy if we are to promote the development of a more integrated approach to landscape and urban planning. Green infrastructure projects that have been deemed successful, for example the London Olympic Park, the High Line in New York or the Cheonggyecheon Stream Restoration Project in Seoul, South Korea, have worked, in part, due to the level of detail, knowledge and local understanding that has been integrated into these developments. These included cross-disciplinary design teams made up of ecologists, arborists, urban designers and water engineers working with nature to retrofit or integrate green infrastructure into high-density or urban areas. Moreover, if we assess the redevelopments of Maggie Daley Park in Chicago or Herrington Country Park in Sunderland, UK, we see the importance of consultation with planning professionals, as well as extensive engagement with the public, i.e. the end users, in successful project work. Where such depth of information can be gathered, we can identify a much finer level of detail and reflection between the proposed investment and the local context – essential aspects of investments in effective green infrastructure. However, where there has been a lack of time or consultation, for example as shown in commentary regarding the Sabarmati Riverfront redevelopment in Ahmedabad (Gujarat, India), projects have been described as failing to meet local needs.

The creation of a multi-disciplinary approach to green infrastructure is therefore considered to be an essential component for effective investment. During its infancy, in the early 2000s, green infrastructure thinking was relatively isolated within the field of land use planning. However, from about 2005 onwards, we witnessed an expansion of the number of advocates and organisations working with green infrastructure, which ranged from landscape and green space planners to wider built environment, economic and socially minded practitioners. This enabled green infrastructure debates to transcend the disciplinary confines of landscape planning and be promoted as a more mainstream policy mandate. Within the UK, England's Community Forests (2004), Countryside Agency (2005) and Natural England (2009) led this process, which has subsequently been taken on by the Landscape Institute and Town and Country Planning Association (TCPA) (2012). The Conservation Fund was an equally instrumental advocate of this process in the USA, and globally in the eyes of many commentators.

Led by the work of Mark Benedict and Ed McMahon (2006), the Conservation Fund expanded the parameters of green infrastructure thinking to engage engineers, hydrologists, conservation professionals and the public in order to promote a more extensive understanding of the concept. Thus, we now see a growing number of professions, for example health and well-being practitioners, housing developers and business improvement specialists, engaging with the concept, enabling it to gain increased prominence.

The ways in which green infrastructure is developed are also being shaped by the scalar nature of landscape resources, and how these can be embedded in policy. Green infrastructure can be found at all scales across our urban and rural landscapes. It is not physically constrained by the limitations of legislative or administrative boundaries, for example city boundaries or electoral wards, as river catchments, forests and nature reserves function at the landscape scale. Furthermore, whilst it is essential to consider the landscape scale when assessing the functionality of green infrastructure, for example in the ongoing discussion of the proposed pan-European forest or the Great North Forest in the UK, it is important to ensure that localised knowledge of landscape functionality is also included. Research being carried out in the Chesapeake Bay area in Maryland is one example where working at a landscape scale has been critical in discussions of ecological functionality. In its green infrastructure work the Conservation Fund has helped to protect 400 acres of forest and riparian habitat along the Savage River in Maryland, whilst on the Chester River, it has collaborated with landowners, the Maryland Department for Natural Resources (DNR), Queen Anne County and the US Fish and Wildlife Service to ensure the protection of 8 square miles of wetlands. It also attracted US$527,000 to restore a 1000-foot stretch of the Kingstowne Stream in Alexandria, Virginia, through investment in dry retention ponds, ecological riverside buffers, meadows and plunge pools to help reduce water and ecological pollution and manage storm water more effectively. All of the above have been linked to the multi-partner Chesapeake Bay restoration project that is using green infrastructure to improve the functionality and quality of the landscape.

A significant proportion of green infrastructure research has therefore focussed on the management of nature, green spaces and parks in neighbourhoods. Although this may seem to limit the transferability of findings due to the localised focus, it does provide a body of evidence, held by organisations such as the TCPA and Natural England, which promotes the benefits that green spaces provide in urban areas. This includes reflections on the viability of green walls and roofs in urban areas, and the value that small pocket parks can add to the use and attractiveness of public space, for example in the Thames Bridge area of London. The middle ground in this argument can be found in the greenways and ecological networks, such as the 606 Greenways and Bloomingdale Trail in Chicago and the Vancouver Greenway Network. These cross urban/rural boundaries, using urban-fringe areas as the location for activity and functionality.

As discussed above, 'multi-functionality' is the key principle that green infrastructure planning aims to deliver. Multi-functionality is considered as the provision of several activities or processes in one location working simultaneously to provide social, economic and ecological benefits, as identified in Central Park. Whilst landscapes do not have to deliver social, economic and ecological benefits in each location, green infrastructure thinking does promote the view that within a network of green spaces, a range of benefits drawn from these three areas will be created, enhanced and maintained. For example, in London the city's wider 'green grid' is made up of neighbourhood (Windmill Gardens and Rush Common in Brixton) and city-scale parks (Clapham Common) that provide benefits for different groups of people, and help to meet local and strategic environmental targets, as set out in the London Plan. These three sites are located within the same area of south London but provide complementary local, district and city-level benefits. The development of a multi-functional landscape linked to a connective network of green space that provides access to nature, and is managed through a multi-disciplinary approach to investment, is therefore a central component of our understanding of what green infrastructure is or should be. However, to apply this thinking in practice requires us to once again reflect on what green infrastructure actually is.

The most frequently reported landscape elements associated with green infrastructure planning are trees (street trees, woodlands and urban forests), water bodies (rivers, urban water bodies, lakes and the reactions to change in these resources due to changing storm water/water systems), urban green spaces (parks, gardens and public spaces), technical-based green infrastructure (green walls, green roofs and sustainable urban drainage systems) and landscape-scale sites (ecological networks and water catchment areas). These resources provide benefits at different scales, which change over time as the landscape evolves, as well as socio-cultural benefits for health, recreation and economic growth needed within society, and as such are used to address a multitude of landscape issues. They also provide options for planners, developers, architects and the public to think about investments in landscape enhancement, as they are useful in various development contexts.

—

Where has green infrastructure come from?

The establishment of a set of grounded principles for green infrastructure owes a debt to the research and landscape practice conducted into greenways, landscape ecology, sustainable communities and more recently ecosystem services and NBS. Each of these areas of planning has influenced how planners, designers and the public interact with the landscapes around them. Consequently, we could argue that green infrastructure is simply the most recent articulation of green space ideas that have influenced the management of the landscape in Europe, North America and Asia. The following provides a more detailed description of a section of these key themes that can be used to contextualise where, why and how we use green infrastructure.

Classical gardens in China

There are clear links between garden design, which reflects traditional interpretations of the physical landscape, and the ways in which humans interact with nature. Variations in height, water, depth (using buildings and windows) and surfaces (i.e. rock, grasses and plants) have all been used to replicate the ethereal nature of large landscape paintings and stories in

←
Humble
Administrator's
Garden
(Suzhou).

←
Lujiazui Park
(Shanghai),
China.

confined urban spaces. The classical gardens of Suzhou (Jiangsu Province, China), as discussed in more detail in a case study in Chapter 3, are examples of this phenomenon and, along with the canals in the old parts of the city, have been classified as a World Heritage Site based on depictions of East Yangtze River Delta garden design (eleventh- to nineteenth-century). Other examples include the Old Summer Palace in Beijing, Keyuan Garden in Guangdong Province and Liyuan Garden in Wuxi, which all use the basic elements of rock, water, flora and fauna, and human interactions with nature to create gardens that are deemed to be nationally and, in many cases, internationally important. Contemporary Chinese green infrastructure has retained several of these elements, yet has also moved towards more western approaches to landscape architecture, for example Lujiazui Park in Pudong, Shanghai, which employs both classical and western styles simultaneously. However, despite this cultural shift, there remains a strong socio-cultural attachment to traditional or classical styles in Chinese green infrastructure planning.

Greenways

Whilst the classical gardens of China have a 2000-year history, the creation of urban green space in western countries, such as the UK and the USA, is far more recent. Following the establishment of Birkenhead Park in 1847, as the first park accessible to all without an entrance fee, there has been a surge in discussions regarding the value of green spaces to the wider public. This manifested itself in the creation of Victorian parks in the UK (1830s–1910s), in the Haussmann-inspired redesign of Paris using boulevards and country vistas (1853–1870), and through the designs of landscape architect Frederick Law Olmsted in the creation of landmark sites in New York, Boston and Montreal (1857 onwards). One aspect of this process in North America was the creation of greenways, which are linear routes between urban and rural areas offering recreational opportunities for people to more easily engage with the landscape. Greenway thinking drew on the parkway movement: parkways were long-distance highways that allowed car owners to drive into areas of scenic beauty for recreation, facilitating engagement with spaces outside cities, whilst greenways provided access to amenities that people could reach on foot or by bicycle. The legacy of greenways can be seen in state-level projects in New England and Florida and city-scale regeneration projects such as the Indy Greenways network in Indianapolis and the Atlanta BeltLine Greenway. Greenways have also been seen to provide a catalyst for investment in urban green spaces, as well as the longer-term management of these spaces, for example the economic uplift associated with the High Line in New York or Olmsted's Emerald Necklace in Boston. Moreover, the ongoing success of the Central Park Conservancy in New York and the prestige of the Parc du Mont-Royal in Montreal

←
Boston
Common and
the Emerald
Necklace, USA.

→
Urban greening
in London, UK.

illustrates the added socio-economic value that greenways
hold in large urban areas, as they remain influential examples
used to shape current landscape planning practice.

Garden cities and sustainable communities

As the influence of greenways and Olmsted facilitated a change
in approach to landscape planning in North America, Ebenezer
Howard's 'Garden City' movement achieved comparable prestige
in the UK. Howard's focus was on the creation of places that were
accessible and functional, yet blended town and country, to help
to alleviate health and socio-economic disparity. His drive was to
address inequality through investment in green infrastructure
and focussed on the creation of small (fewer than 36,000
residents) garden cities that would encompass employment,
homes and community facilities. This would reduce the need
to drive, and thus increase the accessibility of services and
amenities to all members of the community. Whilst only a handful
of garden cities were created in England due to financial and land
ownership constraints, Howard's ethos remains in the TCPA's
calls for investment in garden cities, and its support for green
infrastructure. We can identify Howard's ongoing legacy,

as in 2017 the UK government announced it would be supporting the development of 14 new 'garden villages' and three 'garden towns' that will deliver over 48,000 homes and be based on the Garden City principles. Ebbsfleet in Kent was also identified as a new 'garden city' in 2016 and will combine 45,000 square metres of commercial space with 15,000 new homes and investment in green infrastructure.

Ecosystem services and Nature-Based Solutions (NBS)

More recently, we have seen a shift within planning to integrate more specific, technical, ecological and nature-based language into green infrastructure thinking. Increasingly the processes associated with 'ecological systems' have been addressed in development debates. The promotion of 'supporting', 'provisioning' and 'regulating' services within investment plans has been viewed by many as a way to ensure that the functionality of the landscape, i.e. water systems and biodiversity, is not harmed by development. The UK Natural Ecosystem Assessment (UK NEA, 2011) offers a good guide to the intricacies of ecosystem service approaches. The Queen Elizabeth Olympic Park in London is a successful example of ecosystem services in action. The park's design reflects the fluctuation of water resources on the River Lea and incorporates a sustainable drainage system to help regulate localised and seasonal flooding by promoting periodic flooding of specific parkland located next to the river. Our understanding of these systems provides scope for more specific ecological expertise to be aligned with socio-economic thinking for construction, which may previously have been limited. More recently, we have seen an extension of this process focussing on the development of NBS. NBS promote a more holistic approach to investment that uses 'natural solutions' to help manage landscapes. However, the role that humans play in developing, managing and using the environment must be acknowledged for effective green infrastructure planning when using NBS. Several cities across Europe, and more recently in the UK, are engaged in NBS investment. For example, Manchester City Council and academics from the University of Manchester are looking at using natural systems to develop adaptive flood mitigation and air pollution control in the east of the city. In Liverpool the city council is delivering the EU-funded URBAN GreenUP project and investing in street trees, sustainable drainage and an increased use of pollinator species to address flooding, urban heat island and biodiversity issues.

As discussed above green infrastructure is a continuation of several landscape and environment planning practices that have developed over a number of years. Using Howard and Olmsted as figureheads has helped generate consensus between green infrastructure advocates and has encouraged a more effective approach to landscape planning. Moreover, the lineage between classical and modern garden design in China, and to a lesser extent between older and more recent landscape design in the UK and Europe, is still visible in contemporary development, as is the promotion of human-environmental interactions proposed by Howard in the plans for sustainable communities in London (UK), Davis (USA), and Chandigarh and Gandhinagar (India). What we are seeing, therefore, is a refinement of these approaches aiding green infrastructure advocates to address more localised and current development issues.

↑
The New York
Highline, USA.

→
The proposed
site of the
Camden
Highline, UK.

← Advert for property in Chennai, India.

The socio-economic and ecological benefits of green infrastructure

The creation of multiple benefits associated with green infrastructure is a key delivery goal for investment in landscape resources. Through the provision of green spaces that contain, for example opportunities to interact with the landscape using play equipment or benches in a city park, green infrastructure can utilise NBS and other built infrastructure to establish value for different users. Likewise, we can identify economic values that green infrastructure delivers, for example in real-estate uplift in Hong Kong, the decreased costs of urban flooding in Sheffield and, in Hamburg, lowering the number of doctor visits as health improves with the use of parks. The design of our urban landscapes could also be seen as an important 'branding' exercise for a city, which can have a significant impact on its socio-economic future, as noted in Chennai, India.

Investment in green infrastructure has been shown to deliver significant benefits to individual and communal health, controlling conditions such as asthma and obesity, and by providing spaces that aid memory and physical interactions with nature for people who experience mental health issues such as dementia. The findings of the Mersey Forest's 'Natural Health Service' in Cheshire saw a 40 per cent increase in physical activity and a 20 per cent increase in self-reported well-being across its 3000 participants following engagement with the programme.

In addition, several studies from Scandinavia highlighted an increase in attainment in schools by children who use natural areas as part of their learning environment. This research has been successfully applied in the UK through the delivery of 'Forest Schools', the provision of outdoor learning and play, and the integration of environmental issues into the school curricula. We can also identify improved social well-being and inclusion in older people and members of Black-Asian-Minority Ethnic (BAME) groups when these groups have access to green and open spaces that offer affordances for social interaction. CABE Space's assessment of the added social value of parks in their 'The Value of Public Space' (2003) report provides a series of examples illustrating these discussions. Furthermore, whilst improvements in social cohesion might appear to be minor, within some south Asian city parks, such as in Parimal Gardens in Ahmedabad, India, the role of the space as a communal meeting place is central to both physical and social well-being.

Economically, we can also identify an increase in house prices when homes are located near to parks and high-quality green and blue spaces. Evidence from North America, Europe and South-East Asia suggests that increases in house prices could exceed 20 per cent. Moreover, when homes are located in attractive landscapes, we see a corresponding increase in rental prices and an improved uptake of commercial premises. Maggie Daley Park in central Chicago is one example of this relationship, as it helps to generate an increased local income, which can benefit private enterprise, as well as local housing, business or tourist taxes. There is evidence from the UK and the USA that office and business park green infrastructure can help to increase worker productivity by lowering absenteeism and increasing productivity. Investing in green infrastructure can also improve the quality of life of employees individually, leading to a healthier, happier and more productive workforce.

We can also identify significant ecological benefits when investing in green infrastructure. These include the management of water resources through improvements to individual properties using bioswales and nature-based drainage systems designed to concentrate or filter debris and pollution out of surface water runoff, to wider city-scale improvements in porous paving (areas that use mesh grids of grass to allow water to filter through to subsoils rather than being retained as surface water) and sustainable drainage systems (SuDS) (water sensitive designs that are used to capture, hold and release water during peak flows using natural elements such as grasses, retention ponds and watercourses or rain alleys). We see improved climatic adaptability where street trees are used, especially in countries with monsoonal climates such as India or Malaysia. Trees help to regulate rainfall, but also act as interceptors of air pollutants and moderate the impacts of increased urban heat island associated with traffic fumes and high-density urban form. Urban greening provides habitats for a variety of bird, insect and mammal species, crucial to the existence of urban pollinators which help to ensure that cities continue to be biodiverse environments. Finally, green infrastructure holds political benefits for politicians and decision-makers. Where environmental resources are managed effectively, they become well used and valued by the public, businesses and politicians. The completion of the Cheonggyecheon Urban Design Restoration project in Seoul illustrates the positive responses generated from the public and businesses in terms of increased use and time spent in the city centre (and thus increased economic spend). Therefore, the protection of the natural environment can be a vote winner, as there is less negative publicity if or when a city government is seen to be protecting its environment. It can also provide a competitive advantage for a city: green city indexes focussing on quality of life and place, for example those developed by Siemens AG (2011), have been shown to be influential in business decision-making. Those city officials who can effectively market their green infrastructure as part of their branding, as seen in Singapore and Vancouver, can thus promote themselves as being more competitive compared to other cities.

—

Summary

The chapter has outlined several key principles that are being used to shape how we discuss, research and develop green

↑
SuDS
developments in
Chicago, USA.

→
SuDS
developments in
Berlin, Germany.

infrastructure. These include reflections on scale, the scope of
investment, our changing understanding of the landscape over
time and the different ways in which people engage with green
infrastructure in policy and practice. Each of these principles
will be debated further through the examples and case studies

←
Parks in Berlin,
Germany.

←
Public green
space in
Liverpool, UK.

presented in the following chapters to highlight both the
complexity, and the complementarity of the approaches to
investment in green infrastructure taken across the world.
These chapters focus on where good practice can be identified,
highlighting how it could be replicated in other locations.
They also look at the design, development and management
of investment and illustrate the value of context, landscape
expertise and the vision of advocates in our discussions of and
investments in green infrastructure.

Chapter 2

**What Does Green Infrastructure
Do for Us? Connectivity, Access
to Nature and Establishing
Multi-functionality**

How we create and interact with green infrastructure is central
to our understanding of its value. By investing in green and blue
spaces we can develop a network of sites that support
connectivity and access to nature, as well as promoting multiple
uses for a range of user groups. A key aspect of successful
investment is ensuring that people are engaged with the
landscapes around them, as it is through exposure and
interaction that they start to place social values on the spaces
and subsequently become attached to them. For example,
children who spend a significant amount of time playing outside
are more likely to develop an appreciation of nature than those
who play indoors (see Louv's *Last Child in the Woods* for a more
detailed discussion of this issue). How people and nature are
intertwined influences how we interact with green infrastructure
and is important in showing planners, designers and landscape
professionals how the design and management of environmental
resources can promote functionality. Moreover, although we
could argue that simply creating a network of connected green
infrastructure may lead to use due to its proximity to homes
and places of work, we need to also consider that a better
understanding of people's behaviour enables us to create
more attractive and used spaces (see also Kaplan and Kaplan,
The Experience of Nature: A Psychological Perspective).

This chapter discusses how the physical and psychological
linking together of green spaces has been proposed as a way of
connecting people with the places around them to promote a
better quality of life. Reflecting on the physical composition of
green infrastructure – its location, its aesthetic qualities, as well

as its ability to allow access to nature, especially in urban areas – can ensure lifelong interactions with the environment. Through a discussion of how green infrastructure networks can facilitate changes in behaviour, we can better understand how people value the landscapes around them.

—

Establishing nature as a part of 'place' for people
Nature is an essential element of a liveable, functional and attractive urban area. Many cities around the world have been identified within Green City Indices as using nature as a key selling point of their marketing. Locations including Vancouver, Stockholm and Melbourne are all regularly discussed as being liveable based partially on the quality of their environments with green infrastructure in all its forms being a significant aspect of this valuation. Conversely, cities with a lower level of green infrastructure coverage, less public open space and a greater proportion of built infrastructure, such as the expanded cities of China and India, are viewed less positively.

Establishing nature as a key infrastructure in urban development is therefore seen as being vital in supporting socio-economically liveable cities. The creation of a network of green spaces that promotes interactions between people and the environment is a key component of this process. Richard Louv discussed the role of landscape as facilitating a 'love' of or relationship with the natural environment in his book *Last Child in the Woods* (2005). Environmental 'affordances' in Louv's work are interventions, which allow different people to interact with the same space in diverse ways due to variation in the design and sensory nature of a site. In his work, he argued that designing landscapes that were exciting, interactive and usable for children, individuals, families and the elderly could be considered to provide affordances. If such places can be created then people would want to spend time in a green space, and subsequently would have a longer-term attachment to them. The South Bank riverfront in London is an example of this process. It can be seen as a tourist attraction, a recreational space, an arts venue or an urban greenway linked to the river and surrounding parks, all of which allow people to interact with the site in their own way. Louv and authors such as Joan Nassauer (1995) and Yi-Fu Tuan (1977) have suggested that when nature is part of people's everyday lives they (a) will potentially use it, (b) will value it and (c) will protect it from overdevelopment or exploitation. The master planning of the Queen Elizabeth Olympic Park by the London Organising Committee for the Olympic and Paralympic Games (LOCOG), LDA Design, the Greater London Authority (GLA) and local authorities in London drew heavily on these ideas to create a space that has become part of London's DNA.

However, 'designing in nature' is not necessarily an easy process in the planning of our cities, as shown in the development and adoption of the Gloucestershire Wildlife Trust and University of the West of England's 'Building with Nature' benchmarking toolkit. There is an ongoing debate within the academic, and specifically within the practitioner and construction, literature asking whether it is feasible to require green infrastructure to be a statutory form of infrastructure investment. It also questions what types and proportions of green and blue space are needed and where. Currently, nature remains an 'added extra', which is developed once the key issues of housing, economic development, transport and other infrastructure provision are addressed. This is surely counter-intuitive: green and blue spaces are elements of the landscape that provide us with additional health, well-being and socio-economic benefits. There is, however, a growing evidence base in guidance notes of strategies, for example, highlighting the value of urban nature in our understanding of space and place. This can be seen in the new town of Cambourne in Cambridgeshire, where green space, lakes, waterways and gardens have been integrated into the town's design to provide its residents with access to nature, play spaces and locations to interact with neighbours and friends.

Case Study

London's green space network

As a major global city, London can often seem too dense, too polluted and lacking in public spaces. Oxford Street in central London has been cited as one of the most polluted streets in the world; in February 2018 the city's air quality targets were exceeded (though this was seen as an improvement, as in 2017 the same targets had been exceeded by January). However, approximately 49 per cent of London's area is green infrastructure, which includes the River Thames, the London Wetlands centre and its numerous waterways/river courses. London is also circled by the Metropolitan Green Belt (approximately 516,000 hectares), which provides a wide range of social and recreational, ecological and economic benefits to the city and the wider south-east of England. Breaking down the 49 per cent of green and open space in London into smaller areas, we can identify that London has a significant number of Victorian parks located across the city, which complement its Royal Parks. The city also has a wealth of pocket parks that link neighbourhoods together and form an integral part of London's green space network. These include parks in Bloomsbury, Camden, Chelsea and Lambeth.

More recent investments in pocket parks, allotments and urban greening projects has been seen as helping to actively engage communities around London Bridge, Hackney and Brixton with nature, as well as providing food-growing activities to groups who may be otherwise excluded from such events. Food-growing activities, such as orchards and community gardens, have been successfully developed in Brixton on the main A23 Brixton Hill Road and in the Better Bankside area by the Business Improvement District (BID). In addition, London has invested heavily in its green infrastructure network via the strategic management of the All London Green Grid (ALGG), the Queen Elizabeth Olympic Park in Stratford, around King's Cross/Kings Place in central London, and within the development plans for Nine Elms on the south bank of the River Thames. Each of these investments has seen a substantial improvement in the proportion of green space and an increased understanding of how linking people with green infrastructure through connective features can improve the access opportunities that residents and visitors have to the city's landscapes.

However, there is a parallel debate regarding whether the current management and development proposals for the city's green spaces will deliver benefits to communities, as well as asking whether they can meet the more strategic climate change, air pollution and flooding needs of London. Such considerations have led to a new wave of smaller and innovative projects being developed, some of which are coordinated by the GLA and local borough authorities but others by environmental and community groups, for example Sustain or Groundwork

↑
London's green infrastructure network.

London, groups who are looking to reuse redundant space in London to create new green infrastructure resources. In addition, projects in locations including Camden and Peckham are currently in progress that aim to reuse urban rail infrastructure to create spaces that pay homage to the High Line in New York.

Innovative investment in green infrastructure is counterbalanced by ongoing privatisation of some public spaces, which restricts the use of the city's green infrastructure for its residents. The cordoning off of large parts of Hyde Park, Finsbury Park and Clapham Common to hold music or recreational events is an example of commercialisation activities considered by some local people to detract from the everyday value of the parks. There is also ongoing discussion as to whether any loss of green infrastructure, for example the release of Green Belt land or the removal of London plane trees and a local park on the south bank of the River Thames associated with the now revoked 'Garden Bridge' development, should be minimised. Therefore, although London has a historical green space network that is considered by many as world-leading, there are questions over how the city will develop and manage its green infrastructure in the future.

▬

Green infrastructure as connective elements

The linkage of key green infrastructure resources is a key idea that runs through all discussions of its development and management. How we view green and blue space spatially is important as it provides us with an understanding of what resources exist and where they are, how they complement each other, and crucially where gaps exist in the networks that we can try to address (see Fig. 2.1). Visually this can be a relatively simple process as maps and aerial photographs show us the different types of land use located across a given area. Consultants or local planning authorities normally hold land use maps that can be used to help discuss possible green infrastructure investment (see the Greater Manchester Spatial Framework, the draft London Plan section on green infrastructure, or Cambridgeshire Green Infrastructure Strategy (2011) for examples). However, the usefulness of these resources and their supportive, regulating and provisioning functions associated with ecosystem services needs further enquiry if we are to get the right kinds of trees, plants, park or water management projects in the right place. What is certain, though, is that over the last decade landscape professionals, designers and decision-makers have consistently promoted the connective elements of green infrastructure within their planning and management of urban and rural landscapes.

How the landscape 'fits' together can also be discussed in terms of landscape ecology principles. The theory of landscape 'mosaics' identifies how different land uses can be, and are, located within a given environment providing scope for plant, animals and bird species to move between different areas. However, where landscapes become fragmented due to investment in housing, transport or commercial infrastructure, such as in many North American cities, we can see habitats becoming increasingly isolated. Consequently, the resources needed to support an ecological community can become scarce. This is seen in areas where isolated woodlands exist in large arable landscapes or small wetlands are located in built-up areas, for example the Walthamstow Wetlands in London. The Manchester Airport City extension is a further example of this process, where the fragmentation of ancient woodlands is leading to the destruction of important habitats that link the city and its green belt area.

Within landscape ecology, fragmentation can be addressed through the provision of connective elements: links, hubs and nodes. Links are linear landscape features, for example river corridors, footpaths or migration corridors such as hedgerows and street trees, which are used to connect hubs and nodes. Hubs and nodes are areas of more substantial ecological resource, e.g. a meadow or woodland. The value of links, hubs and nodes within green infrastructure is that they provide a spatial form that promotes movement, interaction and supportive activities between natural resources, people and the landscapes around them. For example, in 1947 the 'Finger Plan' of Copenhagen was approved, which utilises a series of linear features, the 'fingers', to provide green corridors that emanate from the city centre to the suburbs. Housing and other infrastructure has been developed in the sections between the fingers. Elsewhere, Stockholm uses a series of 'landscape islands' and green wedges to connect the city and its outer areas. We can also identify a comparable process in Manhattan where Central Park, Highbridge Park and Riverside Park act as anchor 'hubs', whilst the Manhattan Waterfront Greenway helps to link this site to the smaller parks or nodes, such as Bryant, Union Square and Sara D. Roosevelt parks, across the borough.

To aid connectivity we can therefore identify a range of connective elements used within green infrastructure practice ranging from public footpaths promoting 'nature walks' around urban areas to landscape-scale features such as the state-level greenways in Florida in the USA or green belt designations in South Korea. Each of these elements can be considered to use the landscape to connect different people or ecological communities at a broader scale, thus addressing the isolation of smaller resources. Some of these features are extensive tracts of the landscape and make use of natural elements such as river corridors or established walking trails in national parks, whilst others are more discreet and could be used to facilitate connectivity between habitats only metres apart. The connective nature of landscape ecology and thinking, such as in Ian McHarg's seminal work *Design with Nature*, therefore lends itself to being applied within green infrastructure thinking.

Connectivity is also a key concept in planning, as planners work spatially and use networks to promote interactions between people and the economy. Green infrastructure can be thought of as working in a comparable way. By identifying a network of ecological elements within a landscape, green infrastructure advocates look for the most effective way to link resources to maximise their ecological potential, similar to Ebenezer Howard's promotion of Garden City ideals. Investments in urban greenways such as the Jubilee Greenway in London or the inclusion of tree-lined boulevards in Paris are two examples which use connective routes to promote the movement of people through urban environments.

In addition, there is a wealth of discussion reflecting the role of water as a connective green infrastructure. Canals, rivers and lakes are essential elements of our environmental network as they provide us with drinking water and resources for commercial, industrial and agricultural use. However, larger water bodies can also support economic development and recreational activities, for example Jacqueline Onassis Lake in Central Park in New York. Moreover, in Ahmedabad (India) the city's authorities have planned for the maintenance of its lakes system through a water sensitive approach to the management of flooding and drought situations using sustainable drainage and provision of new green spaces. They have also invested extensively in the Sabarmati Riverfront redevelopment creating a 10-mile public walkway along the river (to date approximately £134 million has been invested in the site). The use of water resources to promote public engagement with the landscape has been a key development priority of the Ahmedabad Municipal Corporation (AMC) and the Ahmedabad Urban Development Authority (AUDA). We can also identify that canals and former industrial waterways, such as those in Liverpool, Manchester and Leeds in the UK promoted by the Canals and Rivers Trust and in European cities such as Amsterdam (The Netherlands) or Stuttgart (Germany), can be used to promote walking, cycling and other recreational activities, as they link people more effectively with the landscapes around them.

Cambridgeshire – a front runner of green infrastructure guidance

Cambridgeshire was a front runner in the development of green infrastructure policy and was one of the first areas in the UK to modify its land use planning practices to consider green infrastructure. This was seen in the creation of the initial Cambridgeshire Sub-Regional Green Infrastructure Strategy produced in 2005. Between 2009 and 2011 the LPAs of Cambridgeshire, the quasi-governmental body Cambridgeshire Horizons and key environment sector agencies came together to revise this initial strategy and articulate their vision for the green and blue spaces of Cambridgeshire. The second strategy gave prominence to the region's city and country parks, its wildlife corridors and habitats, and its network of waterways including the Ouse, Nene and Cam rivers. Each was promoted as an essential connective element within the urban–rural landscape of Cambridgeshire.

The strategy also proposed using a series of landscape-scale ecological 'hubs' in the form of the Great Fen and Wicken Fen projects (managed by the Wildlife Trust and National Trust respectively), and investments in country parks in Ely, Cambourne and Huntingdon to fill in the 'missing links' in the area's strategic green infrastructure network. This included reviewing the existing Rights of Way, cycle paths and canals to promote movement between the wider fen landscape and its urban areas, for example Cambridge and Huntingdon. These spaces were also identified as critical components of the wider Cambridgeshire ecological network allowing migrating birds, insects and mammals to feed, nest and move across the area.

The revised strategy also proposed a hierarchy of investments in green infrastructure, which identified projects that had regional, city and local significance. This was done to ensure that all locations in the area would see investment in their green infrastructure network providing new or enhanced resources. In East Cambridgeshire, this included an investment of £1 million for Ely Country Park (a site of significant district importance), market town greening and the use of strategic waterways for biodiversity enhancement. Moreover, Cambridgeshire as a whole, and specifically the city of Cambridge and the District Councils of Huntingdonshire and South Cambridgeshire, were identified as key sites for strategic development. Whilst in many locations this could have led to conflicts between land uses, within the green infrastructure strategy these locations were considered as key opportunities to support investments in green space provision, such as

Trumpington Meadows in Cambridge providing connective elements between these urban extensions and into the wider network of spaces. The area was also a recipient of central government development funding in the form of the Housing Growth Fund (HGF), which was used with other UK- and EU-level funding (and local capital) to invest in green infrastructure across the region.

—

Promoting access to nature in urban areas

Promoting access to and interactions with nature is central to green infrastructure planning. As discussed previously, those who engage with nature have the benefit of better health, as well as social interaction. Louv also states that this instils a lifelong understanding that being 'in nature' is something that is beneficial for us. Louv's work extends the research of Rachel and Stephen Kaplan, who have debated the restorative value of the landscape. Their work has been used to frame the discussions of attainment of school children, the productivity of office workers and the recovery times of patients in hospital where these groups can interact with or can see nature. Whilst the aesthetics of a landscape have been discussed as a key driver of interaction, see for example the work of Yi-Fu Tuan, *Space and Place* (1977), what Louv outlines is that a location, its amenities and how we access the landscape are all factors that attract people to use green spaces. The notion that people become attached to nature through engagement should therefore be central to how we plan and manage our landscapes. This is particularly important in urban areas where access to space, the quality of these spaces and the amenities they provide can either promote or hinder use. For example, the ongoing discussions of the architecture of housing projects in New York, south Chicago and the Thamesmead estate in London highlight the difficulties we have seen in creating access to parks in large-scale housing developments. We can also argue that achieving successes in this area is part of the wider place-keeping agenda promoted by Dempsey, Smith and Burton (2014), who assessed the ways in which green spaces can be managed to continue to attract users.

However, many large urban areas, for example New York or Shanghai, have appeared to be systematically converting their

→
Green space
in Ahmedabad,
India.

→
Art and green
space in
Vancouver,
Canada.

environmental resources to provide land for housing, commercial
and industrial development, and transport infrastructure.
The cost of such actions has been a significant decrease in the
proportion of green infrastructure in urban areas. Consequently,
where parks, green spaces, urban trails and water bodies remain
accessible they can make a substantial impact on the quality of
life of both individuals and communities. Pocket parks, street
tree protection and urban allotments in New York illustrate the
societal benefits that access to neighbourhood-scale green
infrastructure can deliver. They suggest that interaction with

urban nature improves communal interaction, leads to decreased incidences of ill health and provides a stronger set of social bonds between people and their local environment. However, there is an additional issue linked to such change that these spaces may become increasingly oversubscribed due to their limited size. At a city scale we can identify engagement with greenway trails in US cities, such as Davis or Indianapolis, as examples of how access to nature continues to promote active use of the landscape. Moreover, a visit to any well-maintained local park, such as Heaton Park in Manchester, the Jardin de Luxembourg in Paris or Park am Gleisdreieck in Berlin, shows that accessibility and functionality encourage people to use these spaces. The process of accessing nature therefore becomes a routine part of a lifelong engagement with the environment.

One way to ensure that people live and work in close proximity to green infrastructure was developed in the mid-1990s by English Nature (now Natural England) with the creation of a set of parameters establishing the distances people would travel to use a green space. The *Accessible Natural Greenspace Standards* (ANGSt) noted that a five-minute walk was the maximum amount of time it should take a person to reach a local park or green space. The ANGSt went on to note three further time/distance categories, arguing that planners needed to take the accessibility of green infrastructure into account as a critical design element in urban development. Although the ANGSt has been marginalised in the UK by central government there remain those in green infrastructure practice who continue to use a five- to ten-minute timeframe as the maximum distance that people should be from a green space.

As well as the physical distance people will travel to access green spaces there is a corresponding psychological component to this discussion. Access is not simply about the physical act of engaging with a space but also how individuals or communities view the safety of a place. Well used, well lit and well managed parks are more attractive to a wider variety of people. Moreover, parks that provide activities and amenities for a wide range of people, children, families and older communities are more likely to be well patronised. A successful example of this is the Parco

Nord in Milan, which blends sports, urban agriculture, water features and large areas of grasslands into a multi-functional destination park. Conversely, green infrastructure sites that are considered isolated, unwelcoming or unkempt can significantly limit use. Parks can be redeveloped to address such issues, though, with the Jardins d'Eole in Paris one such example. Through a community-led design process and an understanding of how different communities use the site, existing anti-social behaviour was mitigated and a greater sense of community ownership was developed following its reopening in 2007. However, as discussed by CABE Space, we have to be aware that there is an ongoing process of interpretation associated with parks that requires individuals to make judgements on the accessibility of a site, which are not always positive.

Access to nature can thus be seen as a key aspect of use, and can be linked to the understanding of environmental systems discussed in landscape ecology. The roles of footpaths, parks and green belts as links, hubs and nodes within a landscape provide the physical structure of landscape features that can be used to engage people with the environments around them. This is important, as people want to access nature in different ways and from alternative locations. Therefore, to be able to use linear corridors to access larger parks or green spaces provides the landscape with an additional capacity to facilitate use.

—

Case Study **Integrating nature in central Berlin**

Berlin has been renowned as a city of change. After the Second World War, the city was segregated into East and West Berlin leading to the creation of new green infrastructure resources in both sides of the city. Following reunification in 1990 the cityscape of Berlin was reintegrated; whilst retaining the existing wealth of city parks, it also invested in new pocket parks, waterways and urban greening projects. What is apparent from a review of Berlin's green space is the renewal and redevelopment of former industrial or derelict sites throughout the city into parks. Examples of this include the change of use from a commercial airport to a city-scale park at the Park Tempelhofer Feld, a former railway infrastructure site now transformed into a nature park at the Natur-Park Schöneberger Südgelände, and the redevelopment of a former

→
Public parks in
Berlin, Germany.

railyard and industrial buildings into the Park am Gleisdreieck,
which now houses a multi-age play area, a brewery and a variety
of nature/play areas that are accessible by train (SBahn/UBahn)
and foot. We can also identify a growing use of the landscape by
'social cooperatives' to provide access to nature in housing
developments. This is particularly prominent in the former
East Berlin where investment in neighbourhood-scale green
infrastructure has been more limited. These sites provide new
spaces within the city but they also complement the existing
green infrastructure of the Grosser Tiergarten, the parks of
Charlottenburg and the River Spree. The latter has recently
been rebranded as an urban waterfront with accessible beach
and swimming facilities in the summer months. Proximity to
nature therefore comes in many forms in Berlin and allows
people to access the city's landscape at a local and city level.

Case Study

Copenhagen's 'Finger Plan'

As noted previously, Copenhagen has often been held up as an
exemplar of accessibility within green infrastructure planning.
From 1947–8 onwards the city's 'Finger Plan' has been
embedded in successive regional and city plans promoting the
use of green wedges permeating Copenhagen's urban fabric to
provide access to green space. Copenhagen made a conscious
effort to allow the development of grey infrastructure, i.e.
buildings, in non-green finger areas. This is significantly
different to other cities, which plan for green infrastructure in
the spaces left empty following development. Consequently,
Copenhagen has been able to moderate some of the impacts
of urban development through a relatively rigid approach to the
protection of the Finger Plan. In addition to the wider benefits
associated with access to nature derived from the Finger Plan,

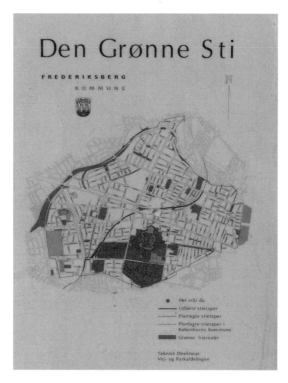

→
Map of
Copenhagen's
Finger Plan in
Frederiksburg,
Denmark.

the city has also invested in neighbourhood parks and greenways, for example in Frederiksburg, to provide the city's population with local options regarding their use of and access to nature. This illustrates how aspects of landscape ecology in the shape of links, hubs and nodes, and the provision of a variety of spaces, can support the long-term investment, management and use of green infrastructure.

___

How does green infrastructure promote multi-functionality?
One role of green infrastructure is to be the location of amenities that provide its users with 'multi-functional' benefits. Multi-functionality is the provision of socio-economic and ecological benefits simultaneously within a given location or across a wider network of green spaces. This could reflect the regulating, provisioning, supporting and cultural services explored within

ecosystems services discussions or it could mean that people have access to a place that they can use in different ways, for different activities and at different times. Multi-functional landscapes are, therefore, varied in their composition, their amenities and their use. This is a benefit for landscape professionals as it allows them to focus their work on specific aspects of greening, and a review of any landscape or urban design competition illustrates the variability of understanding of what green infrastructure can and should look like. However, it can also hinder investment as the range of opportunities can dilute the focus of development in the minds of some planners or decision-makers.

How we define what we consider a 'multi-functional' landscape is shaped by what we as individuals, communities, planners or developers require from a space. Developers will want the maximum economic return from an investment and can use green infrastructure as a way of improving the aesthetic quality of their developments. Developers are, however, also starting to investigate the viability of sustainable drainage systems, additional street greening and the use of urban parks as design features that increase both the amenity value of an area and the economic value of their developments in the market place. This is seen across the word with real-estate investments in Shanghai, Bengaluru (India) and New York where access to high-quality green infrastructure has been employed as a successful marketing tool. In contrast, local governments look to create multi-functional landscapes that help to deliver social inclusion, play/recreation, health and well-being, climate change and urban flood mitigation benefits simultaneously. To do this they look at how green infrastructure can be managed more effectively to deliver the greatest number of benefits, to the widest population, in the most cost-effective way.

Individuals and communities can help shape the process towards multi-functionality in a more nuanced way than a council or developer might. Individuals use places where they gain value. These can include playgrounds for children, sports facilities for all age groups, areas of tranquillity to promote restorative health, or simply benches that allow people to sit down, relax and talk to each other. The NHS, Clinical Commissioning Groups (CCG) and CABE Space have all made direct links between landscape functionality and public well-being in the UK promoting the use of parks to encourage exercise and manage obesity, cardiovascular disease and asthma. In addition, green infrastructure can have a psychological impact derived from the attractiveness, interactivity or perceived safety of a location, such as in the sensory garden in Musgrave Park in south Belfast (UK), which is located next to a hospital.

Likewise, we can identify in communities an emerging consensus regarding what green infrastructure should look like, what services it should deliver and how it should be managed. People like parks, street trees, waterfront and riverfront developments, and local spaces that can be used on a regular basis. They like high-quality spaces that are well managed, proximate to where they live, and which provide opportunities to do different things in the same space. This becomes clearer in cases where green spaces such as parks are threatened with closure or sale. One of the reasons why parks generate such strong feeling is the sense of communal attachment that they help to generate. In some cases, this is a long-term process, for example the long-standing Somali community engagement with Princess and Crown Street parks in Liverpool, older people's use of Parimal Garden in Ahmedabad for their morning yoga classes or the 'wedding corner' in Shanghai's People's Park where mothers go to arrange marriages for their children. There are also attachments to parks and green spaces associated with more recent immigrant populations: Mexican and other Latino communities playing sports in Los Angeles or New York, or refugee communities' use of parks in Sheffield (UK), as they provide free and accessible amenities. Within each of these groups we can identify a range of socio-cultural practices promoting ongoing engagement with the physical landscape linked to gardening, urban allotments and other forms of ecological husbandry providing a mix of environmental, social and ecological benefits.

Each of these types of use shows how green infrastructure resources support multiple functions. This, as already noted, is a key principle of green infrastructure as it provides advocates with a suite of options through which to develop new green and blue spaces. However, it must be acknowledged that multi-functionality is not needed or indeed desirable in all sites, as there may be a significant, e.g. ecological or socio-economic, function associated with that location. In such situations the central function of the site should be supported. In most locations though it is possible and advisable to plan for multiple functions in one site.

Case Study

Liverpool — establishing multi-functionality in the city's green infrastructure

The city of Liverpool historically developed its green space network as a response to the wealth accumulated through the import/export of goods and people (both forcibly and otherwise). As the city became wealthier landowners invested in a series of parks: Sefton, Newsham and Princes circling the city centre. When initially developed, these spaces were private and reserved for landowner use only, but over time as they were gifted, bought or taken into city ownership they have grown to form a significant multi-functional asset to the city. The ring of parks provides formalised green spaces (and their associated amenities) for local people but they also link with public rights of way and cycle routes (such as the city's Loop Line and National Cycle Network) and to other smaller neighbourhood-scale parks. This allows people to access different types of nature in the city, some of which provide more family orientated activities, such as Sefton Park, whilst others are more 'natural' in their management, as at Alt Valley Park. All sites though contribute to the mitigation of climate change in the city, as well as managing surface water flooding.

Questions have been raised, however, asking whether the maintenance of the aesthetic quality of Sefton and Stanley parks, two of the city's Green Flag awarded sites, has limited the ability of Liverpool City Council to fund smaller parks across the city. This has led to debate over the quality of parks in Liverpool with people arguing that some sites offer more benefits than others. Added to this is a discussion of socio-economic/demographic equitability, split roughly north–south across the city in terms of perceptions of poor versus high quality, respectively. This has yet to be resolved but within all parts of the city there is a mix of older and more contemporary spaces (such as Everton Park which was created in the 1980s), which provide amenities for local people. More recently, Liverpool has also looked to develop Public-Private Partnerships (PPPs) to fund new park development. For instance, the development of the Liverpool ONE shopping complex facilitated an investment in Chavasse Park and other urban greening, which has been used to provide additional parkland and improved aesthetic quality to the urban core of the city.

→
Green infrastructure incorporating sustainable drainage in New Orleans, USA.

→
Green space provision on the Thamesmead estate, London, UK.

Maggie Daley and Millennium parks, Chicago

Maggie Daley Park in downtown Chicago is a further example of a park born from a reuse of brownfield land, previously the site of the city's railyards. It was opened in 2014, and the 20-acre site promotes the interaction of people with recreation spaces, places of cultural interest and sports facilities (ice skating and tennis). Millennium Park, adjacent to Maggie Daley, was opened in 2004. Covering an area of 24.5 acres, it provides public space for recreation and the arts through an open-air theatre, with a footbridge that links the park to the Art Institute of Chicago. Both parks offer a range of sporting, artistic and ecologically based activities. However, although the parks sit beside Lake Michigan, they are cut off from it by Route 41 (Chicago South Lake Shore Drive), making their onsite features more valuable to users. One of the key successes of the site has been to integrate social functions for different user groups without creating conflicts between them.

A key design feature of both parks is the partitioning of areas from each other to make unique spaces within the wider parks complex. This has been achieved through careful screening using hedges and trees and the inclusion of pathways, which meander through the park. The outcome

↑
Multi-functional green space, London, UK.

←
Maggie Daley Park, Chicago, USA.

has been a subtler movement of people through the park that allows them to stop and use certain places more fluidly than in parks where the flow of people is one-directional. Given their location both parks are seen as successfully promoting multi-functionality, as they have drawn people back into an underused area of the city centre and enabled them to engage with sports, play, social interaction, and arts and culture. The parks have also shown that investment in green infrastructure is economically viable, as businesses around the parks generate higher incomes because of the increased footfall in the area.

Summary

The majority of green infrastructure investments utilise the principles of access to nature and connectivity to promote a greater engagement between people and the environment, thus establishing 'multi-functional' spaces. This process varies depending on the location, the nature of investment being proposed, and the needs of human and ecological communities. What it delivers is green infrastructure that is physically diverse in size and composition, leading to a range of uses and values being placed upon it. It is therefore important to ensure that such variation exists, as without it there is a likelihood that a green space will only service a small proportion of the possible communities that could benefit from it. In addition, it is important that green infrastructure advocates are aware of how best to ensure that connective landscape elements are embedded within development plans to ensure that nature is accessible. If this is possible then the level of patronage for sites is likely to increase. Moreover, where networks of green spaces are brought together via links, hubs and nodes we see a greater ecological resilience to urban and climatic change, which is important in delivering sustainable urban development. To achieve this takes time and effort from landscape designers, politicians and communities who need to work collaboratively to shape the ways in which green infrastructure is used at both a local and landscape scale.

Chapter 3   **How Do People Interact with Landscapes? Understanding the Value of Green Infrastructure**

Taking the principles and functionality of green infrastructure as a starting point this chapter discusses how different green infrastructure resources in different locations facilitate different interactions and understandings of place. This draws on examples from the UK, North America and China showing how, as already mentioned, the understanding of green infrastructure is culturally defined by our age, gender, ethnicity and experiences. The following discussion therefore reflects upon the complexity of getting green infrastructure right in policy-making, design and management to ensure that people use and appreciate their local/city resource base.

Why do people view green infrastructure differently?
Every person views landscapes as individual collections of elements that they assess against their own experiences, preferences and value systems. These assessments will be influenced by where they were born, where they grew up, where they live and work, and how they have interacted with the landscapes around them. This is not to say that cultural norms all have the same influence on how we 'view' the landscape but it does provide a very personalised basis for discussion. If we subsequently review the wider societal interpretations of nature we can identify additional factors, such as scale, types of green infrastructure and associations with certain activities, which can help us to unravel why we view landscapes differently.

Variation is potentially most prominent in how we view the differences between urban and rural landscapes. This can be dependent on whether you interacted with landscapes as a child, and whether you identify amenity and/or aesthetic values with these locations. If for instance you were raised in rural England, then wider open countryside landscapes and spending time outdoors are normal. However, if you were raised in a city where green infrastructure was confined to formal parks and possibly a river then your understanding and subsequent valuation of the landscape could be very different. Similarly, people who have grown up in cities in North America and those who were raised in rural or coastal areas differ in their understanding of place. We can also expand this notion to an international scale arguing that people born in the UK or USA differ in how they see and value green infrastructure from people raised in New Delhi, Shanghai or São Paulo (Brazil). For individuals raised in urban environments, green infrastructure could mean a pocket park in New York, a cool oasis of urban trees in Shanghai or a spot to be alone with a loved one in New Delhi; all are green spaces but all are used differently. Such a perspective can be seen in urban areas where affordances for play, social interaction and relaxation can make a place functional and liveable.

In contrast, people used to viewing green infrastructure at a landscape scale, for example people raised in rural areas, see greater variation in the form, structure and diversity of animal and bird species over a greater distance. They can identify subtle changes in landscape over larger areas and appreciate the interactions of humans with the environment to a greater extent. The development of national parks in the UK is one example where a wider scale of interpretation is fundamental to the value of these locations. Research engaging with indigenous communities in Australia, West Africa (cf. Fairhead and Leach 1996) and the Pacific North-West of Canada has discussed the notion of landscape perspective as part of their survival mechanism, of communal histories and of landscape education.

What this suggests is that no two people view the landscape in the same way. We can also argue that there are societal norms that we identify within landscapes, especially in the UK and Europe, where specific areas, actions and activities are imbued with literary, artistic and cultural meaning. Indeed, the discussion of the landscape aesthetic in the UK is central to how areas of upland, moorlands and plains are regarded as places of high quality or heritage value. The process of valuation is influenced by nostalgic interpretation of green infrastructure in many places, including Salisbury, which is associated with a painting by John Constable, and the 'Roman' landscapes of Hadrian's Wall in Northumberland on the England–Scotland border. Due to such variation, the nuance of history, arts and social meaning ascribed to the landscape means that when we look at green infrastructure we actually assess the context in which the resources are located, that location within the wider urban/rural landscape and the opportunities for interaction that these spaces offer for people used to different types of environments. Thus, the role of street trees, pocket parks and riverfront promenades may appear to be superfluous to people used to open fields or woodlands, and vice versa. Each of these places though retains a value as part of a suite of options that planners can use when developing investment in green and open spaces. How we explore, examine and value green infrastructure is therefore constructed through a complex understanding of societal and ecological perspectives drawn together into an understanding of place.

Case Study · **Manchester – St Peter's Square**

In 2013 Manchester City Council approved plans to redevelop the city centre square to allow the city's tram network to run smoothly through it. The redevelopment led to significant cosmetic and structural changes to the square and specifically to its Peace Garden, including movement of existing monuments and the demolition of buildings. An open plaza replaced this and although it looks relatively bereft in terms of greenery, the design lends itself to interaction in different ways. What landscaping has been incorporated could be considered to be design-orientated rather than people-orientated. The site does now, however, include several benches, seats and an open public plaza where interaction is possible. Moreover, the design actively promotes interactions with these spaces as they offer affordances to children and adults alike to climb, walk and sit on the benches. When compared to other green spaces in Manchester city centre, such as Piccadilly Gardens, it may not appear to be as welcoming or 'green' but it does serve similar functions for people using the city library, trams and council buildings.

Case Study

Sunderland – Herrington Country Park

Herrington Country Park lies in the urban fringe of Sunderland in the north-east of England. The park is built on a former coal-mining site in the village of Penshaw, overlooked by the locally significant Penshaw Monument. Prior to its creation, the area was a denuded site with little social, ecological or economic value. Since its redevelopment it has become a major visitor attraction due to its fishing and boating lake, sculpture trail, a high level of biodiversity and spaces for people to enjoy multiple activities simultaneously. Furthermore, it now hosts the Durham County Show and other significant events, thus revitalising the site both socially and economically. The development of this urban-fringe site has also promoted a sense of ownership among local people, as suggested by the following apocryphal story told by a member of the local environment community. The story goes that when the country park's trees were first planted they were stolen. However, due to the renewed sense of ownership that the local community felt over the site the perpetrators were advised to return the trees, which they did in the following days. Even in such a short space of time people started to view the site as 'their park' and took pride in the value it had added to their local landscape. This took the form of landscape functionality but was also a recognition that the former 'working' landscape was once again working for the community, in this case as a country park.

North American interpretations of green infrastructure

There is an extensive history associated with interaction, appreciation and modification of the landscape in North America. This is linked to indigenous understanding of nature, mass migrations following immigration, more recent calls to preserve nature in perpetuity and current discussions of the most effective ways to monetise these locations. These debates centred traditionally on wetland, waterways, prairies and mountainous regions, but also reflect upon the ways in which nature has been incorporated into cities in the USA and Canada. The diversity of landscapes in North America coupled with its spatial distribution has made the identification of a single narrative for landscape perceptions difficult. Alternatively, there has been a subtler and regional promotion of landscape understanding that links the rural and urban through a continuum of use and environmental features, such as the way in which the Chicago River in Chicago and Illinois was designed.

Part of this process is reflected in a review of urban development in the USA in the twenty-first century, which highlights a shift away from European-style urban development that favoured variation and diversity in city form. It gave rise to a technical and geometric approach to urban planning that is more prevalent as you move away from the older established cities on the east coast. The new approach was similar to that proposed by the New York planner Robert Moses, who craved uniformity and control over people, their movement and the physical landscape. Within such a controlled regime there are questions on how far green infrastructure can be integrated, as well as how to ensure its multi-functional benefits are delivered. Therefore, although we see continuity in urban form in many mid-western/western cities of the USA there is not necessarily a corresponding investment in green infrastructure. However, within landscape architecture there are remnants of a more flexible approach to development that understands the value of nature within cities. Such variation has allowed more diverse approaches to green infrastructure implementation that utilise river corridors, greenways and the greening of derelict spaces to invest in urban nature. This process is not confined to US cities but is also present in Canada, where parts of Montreal and Vancouver illustrate how green infrastructure can help to revitalise a city, especially when compared to the formulaic design of Winnipeg. Stanley Park in Vancouver and Parc du Mont-Royal in Montreal are two examples of how nature features have been used to facilitate greater interactions and appreciation of the landscape in urban areas.

We can also trace the development of green infrastructure in North America to the growth of personal transport and the use of the motorcar. As cars became affordable and people had more leisure time, parkways were developed to allow citizens to access nature from urban areas. Parkways are considered a forerunner to greenways, which scaled back the spatial extent of parkways and located linear or circular routes within urban areas. This gave free, at the point of use, access to green infrastructure, which could be used for recreation, sports or social interaction. Moreover, greenways provided excellent connective features to link habitats and allow flora and fauna to move around cities. In many places, including Vancouver and New York, the addition of greenways to urban landscapes has been fundamentally important in enabling people to reach outdoor spaces. In recent years, the use of greenways has decreased while spaces that come under the terminology of 'green infrastructure' have become more popular. However, the principles of linearity, access to nature and multi-functionality remain central to investments in urban greening: the Atlanta BeltLine being one of the most recent and high-profile examples of this process.

Current green infrastructure research in North America focuses extensively on a number of discrete areas, namely: biodiversity and conservation, the economic value of green and blue spaces, and the management of water, predominantly storm water. Consequently, we can identify innovation in how ecology and water systems are managed in urban areas in both the USA and Canada, even if this has limited the use of more societal approaches to green infrastructure planning. This has, however, provided cities with a rich set of projects, evidence and data outlining how SuDS, porous pavements, bioswales and discreet household water capture and release systems can make a positive impact on urban water management. Cities in the Pacific North-West have led the field in this regard with Portland and Seattle examining how best to manage their climate. We are also seeing SuDS used in Chicago to moderate rainfall and snowmelt, and in desert locations, such as Phoenix, to manage the limited water resources available. Moreover, the release of PlaNYC, the New York Green Infrastructure Strategy, in 2007 highlighted the added value associated with effective storm water management. PlaNYC outlined a series of interventions in SuDS, habitat recreation and NBS to complement existing engineered infrastructure solutions.

Significant investments were subsequently made in sustainable shorelines on the Hudson River, wetland and fresh water vegetation in the Brooklyn Bridge Park, and an investment of US$2 million in green infrastructure to minimise storm water damage.

In addition to the innovations in storm water management, North American green infrastructure planning is characterised by its approach to landscape management. Researchers and practitioners have embraced landscape-scale ecological conservation practices to ensure that green infrastructure resources including the Chesapeake Bay area of Maryland are managed effectively. Drawing on the principles of landscape ecology, organisations such as the Conservation Fund have pioneered landscape restoration work using the links-hubs-nodes approach to management discussed previously. A further benefit has been the ability of state agencies such as the Maryland and Illinois DNRs to use green infrastructure as a mechanism to generate buy-in from civil and hydrological engineers, real-estate agencies, the environment sector and local government and to encourage these entities to think more critically about how best they can manage their environmental resources and promote sustainable practices.

This is an evolving process that is generating positive responses from stakeholders. However, green infrastructure still requires advocates to promote its inclusion in policy and practice, as it is not yet considered to be an essential infrastructure. The reversal of the flow of the Chicago River is one example where multiple stakeholders were engaged. Through a collaborative partnership between the city, its Metropolitan Water Reclamation District (MWRD), the Army Corps of Engineers and environmental organisations such as Forest Preserves of Cook County, they reversed the flow of the river and created new woodlands and wetlands to accommodate seasonal flooding. The project has delivered significant benefits including reductions in urban storm water flooding, decreased clean-up and insurance costs, increased biodiversity, and the creation of new hiking, cycling and recreational spaces around Chicago.

Boston – managing climate change through historical green infrastructure

Boston's most famous green infrastructure resource is the Frederick Law Olmsted-designed 'Emerald Necklace', a 450-hectare chain of parks, waterways and green spaces that were developed in the mid-late 1800s. Designed to minimise seasonal flooding from the Charles River, the necklace complex stretches from the city centre into neighbourhoods in the west and south of the city. Through a diverse range of landscape features including formal parkland and wetlands the Emerald Necklace ensures that watercourse fluctuations are moderated along its length to limit surface water flooding. In addition to the direct climatic improvements provided by the Emerald Necklace there are additional economic and social benefits derived from the increased access to recreational facilities, increased real-estate prices associated with proximity to the resource, and the provision of an important habitat for urban plant and animal species and migratory birds. Although the Emerald Necklace is the most well-known green infrastructure investment in Boston, the city has also seen major interventions in urban greening on the Central Artery, which was redeveloped as the Rose Fitzgerald Kennedy Greenway. This project converted a multi-lane elevated expressway into a 1.5-mile and 15-acre set of parks and green spaces in the east of the city. The expressway was relocated below ground and the new greenway now offers open-access park space where formerly

←
Boston
Common, USA.

→
Alexandra Park,
Belfast, UK.

→
Connswater
Greenway,
Belfast, UK.

an exclusionary and polluting feature was located. Across
the wider Boston metropolitan area, the Charles River
Watershed Association has also invested in habitat creation
to minimise flooding, as well as providing guidance and
funding for community-scale bioswales, rain gardens and
permeable pavements; all of which, like the Emerald Necklace,
aim to alleviate the negative impacts of surface and storm
water flooding.

European understandings of landscape and green infrastructure
Attitudes to landscape in Europe have been linked directly to
geographical differences and societal interpretations of the
environment. In England, the understanding of green
infrastructure is linked to art and literature and a national idyll
that promotes the peaceful, the pastoral and the rural. In Ireland,
the windswept coastline of Northern Ireland or the Ring of Kerry
in the Republic of Ireland are culturally significant (and now
immortalised in TV and cinema). In parts of central Europe forest
landscapes and their social and ecological value are central to
how people interact with the environment. Whilst in some
north-western European nations, forests are places of solitude
and isolation, in Poland they are locations of community activity
and history. In Scandinavia, waterscapes and rural areas are
popular locations for cultural exchange, vacations and social
interaction. Each of these cultural interpretations of landscape is
grounded in social and historical understanding and highlights
the myriad ways that society has engaged with the environment.
This is no different to how green infrastructure is discussed
across the EU.

In the UK, planning policy is framed to illustrate a need to
respect and manage green infrastructure but fails to provide the
legislation required for its protection. Local governments are
advised to think in accordance with the National Planning Policy
Framework (NPPF) (2012) about how green infrastructure can
be integrated into local development plans but this is not a legal
requirement. The exception is the sacrosanct protection of green
belt designations, which draws on the pastoral view of the UK's
landscape as a time capsule referring back to interpretations
of the English landscape in the 1950s. To address this lack of
policy support it has fallen to environmental advocates to
promote the health, well-being, economic and ecological value
of investment in the landscape. England's Community Forests
and increasingly Natural England, the National Trust and the
Environment Agency have been key advocates in this process.
Moreover, most investment in green infrastructure has been
delivered via the environmental sector, who have worked
extensively with communities, businesses and local government

to ensure landscape resources are developed, funded and managed effectively. This has become increasingly acute due to ongoing austerity policies in the UK, which have limited the funding available from central and local government for investment in green infrastructure.

Compared to the UK many European countries have engaged with green infrastructure more directly within their landscape and urban planning. As noted above, societal connections exist between people and the landscape in central and northern Europe, which reflect historical human-environmental interactions. This is of particular importance in Scandinavia, where spending time in (or with) nature is a normalised part of life for many people, and embedded within the national psyche. Research carried out in Sweden, Denmark and Finland has highlighted the cultural value of engaging with nature for school children and other members of society. Moreover, in cities such as Berlin and Paris we can identity eras of extensive investment in green infrastructure. In Paris, the Haussmann redevelopment of the city created its tree-lined boulevards and many of its parks. Successive governments have extended this process integrating urban greening into the very fabric of the city's arrondissements (districts) through investments in street greening, pocket parks, retrofitting of industrial infrastructure, for example the 55-hectare Parc de la Villette and Promenade Plantée, and larger city-scale sites such as the Bois de Boulogne. Berlin has witnessed a comparable form of green infrastructure development linked to the rise and fall of several governments. This has created the Tiergarten, the repurposing of the Reichstag grounds as public spaces, Tempelhofer Feld and the River Spree as multi-purpose green spaces, and more recently Park am Gleisdreieck which has regenerated a derelict railyard site into a public park and playground serving immigrant and established Berliner communities.

We can identify further variation in Mediterranean countries where green infrastructure has been used alongside traditional architecture to moderate the climate of urban areas. In Italy and Spain, we see examples of how street trees, investment in urban water features and the use of parks enable public spaces to become locations of social interactivity, while managing climatic changes such as heat stress or drought. Although we may not see the same types of plant species or extent of green space as in many northern European countries, landscape designers in southern Europe are increasingly aware of the health benefits offered by green infrastructure and are incorporating urban greening into their designs. The funding and management of green infrastructure across this climatic zone does, however, vary depending on the wider socio-economic standing of a location. However, what is apparent within practitioner and researcher reflections, particularly in Italy, is that green infrastructure can have a positive influence on the social and ecological well-being of a city.

Case Study

Belfast — understanding the place of green infrastructure in urban areas

The city of Belfast has a diverse relationship with its landscape. In many areas of the city, public space has acted as a segregationist marker of community identity, leading to the creation of areas of exclusion. However, Belfast also has a corresponding history of community engagement with green spaces, where communities of all types were active park users before violence become synonymous with the city in the 1960s and 1970s. Conflict linked to 'The Troubles' between Protestant and Catholic communities, the city and the British government and armed forces placed significant restrictions on how green spaces were used. Consequently, large tracts of public space were made redundant, as they were rethought of as 'interface' zones where social interaction became difficult. Since the signing of the Belfast Agreement, also known as the Good Friday Agreement, in 1998, there has been a growing consensus within the city that the landscape can once again be thought of as a place of inclusion, interaction and communal value. This can be witnessed in the growing use of parks and green spaces for recreation, sports and social interaction. Moreover, we are seeing significant investment in the city's waterfront at Laganside and in its parks by Belfast City Council to foster a greater sense of ownership and inclusion. The Belfast Agenda (Belfast City Council, 2007), the city's development plan until 2030, explicitly argues that creating a landscape that is functional, aesthetically pleasing and inclusive is vital to the success of the city's economic and social development.

Investments in green infrastructure include new equipment and security facilities in parks, green walls and roofs, and greater environmental awareness programmes for local communities. However, the implementation of green infrastructure across the city is varied and there are ongoing discussions about the equity of green and open space between different neighbourhoods. Partly this reflects the political tensions of equitable delivery to Protestant and Catholic communities, but it also signals a lack of investment from the private sector in areas of Belfast considered as economically unviable. The exceptions have been the development of the Connswater Greenway, a 10-mile and £40-million investment in connective green and open space features, and the redevelopment of Victoria Park which links the Titanic Quarter with homes in east Belfast, where extensive investment has been made to facilitate play, sports and engagement with the physical landscape. Both projects engaged extensively with communities during the design and management process to ensure long-term buy-in from local people.

Case Study

Sheffield – urban greening promoting urban liveability

Sheffield, like many cities in the UK, has been subject to post-industrial decline which has impacted upon the cohesion of its society, its economic viability and the functionality of its landscape. Despite being England's greenest city in size (36,238 hectares) but not proportion (given the percentage), due in part to the Peak District National Park falling within the city boundary, the urban core of Sheffield has limited green infrastructure. Sheffield is also subject to extensive fluctuation in how its main river, the River Don, flows through the city; in 2007 flooding of the river led to over £1 million pounds of damage and the loss of two lives. To address the potential for further damage Sheffield City Council and the South Yorkshire Community Forest engaged with the EU-funded Interreg IVB project 'Valuing Attractive Landscapes in the Urban Economy' (VALUE) to design, implement and evaluate the role that green infrastructure could play in improving the liveability of the city. Through the VALUE project the city invested in street trees, a new riverside walkway and street furniture on Blonk Street. It also designed four alternative investment scenarios for the Nursery Street zone of the Wicker, an area of significant risk of flooding, looking at the maintenance of the existing landscape, as well as integrating a greater proportion of green infrastructure in the form of a floodable wetland, street trees and a new urban park. The outcome has been a change in the aesthetic quality of the area and an ongoing conversation between the city, residents and local businesses focussing on how best to utilise green and blue spaces to manage the area more sustainably. The foresight shown in this project to address climatic issues with long-term investment in green infrastructure runs counter to the current discussion of the city council's decision to persist with a Public Finance Initiative (PFI) contract that could see hundreds of the city's trees felled to reduce maintenance costs. How Sheffield approaches its long-term management of its environment is therefore still open to debate.

→
Urban greening,
Manchester, UK.

→
Green
infrastructure
in low-income
housing,
Chicago, USA.

→
St Peter's
Square,
Manchester, UK.

→
Green wall,
central Paris,
France.

—

Green infrastructure in a south and east Asian context

Green infrastructure planning has a long history in Asia, especially in China and India. As a nation, China has a cultural attachment to landscape focussing on the elements of water, rock and mountains, as well as placing value on the role people play as managers and consumers of these spaces. The landscape painting of China has been fundamental in shaping the ways in which landscape architecture has been, and is still, practised, with many of the country's most visited attractions taking their design cues from paintings and tapestry created over 1500 years ago. These ideas can be seen in the historical sectors of Shanghai, Hangzhou and Xi'an but are also employed in smaller cities to provide green spaces for people's everyday use. Within each of these cities there is a replication of the classic structure of rock, water and vegetation laid out to convey variation in height, diversity and landscape functionality. Similarly, in India and other parts of south Asia we witness a historical view of the landscape drawn from literature highlighting its role in supporting the Mughals in their approaches to landscape and urban design. Moreover, there is also a strong religious link between landscape and the population of India associated with the seven holy rivers of the country (including Brahmaputra, Ganges and Yamuna), which are linked to public engagement with the environment and social rituals.

In the twentieth century, we see a changing emphasis placed on green infrastructure planning in India and Pakistan to reflect changes in governance and colonial control. The cities of New Delhi and Bengaluru in India and Lahore and Islamabad in Pakistan are examples of how green infrastructure has been employed within civic architecture to provide vital spaces for climate control, water management and social interaction. This includes the provision of maidans (large grassed areas where people congregate) in central areas and large-scale investments in public spaces associated with the colonial urban expansions of government, such as the Secretariat in New Delhi or the provision of green belt areas between sectors of Islamabad.

More recently we can identify the use of urban greening to promote a more contemporary interpretation of popular landscape aesthetics in both India and China. This includes the employment of western landscape architects, the introduction of non-native species and the design of more inspiring parks, promenades and green infrastructure. In many places such as Ahmedabad in India this has been linked to rebranding the city as liveable and economically prosperous, whilst in others it has been used to illustrate a conjoint understanding of landscape history and modernity, such as the Bund and Pudong in Shanghai. What is clear from each of these examples is how the value of landscape remains central to the design, creation and management of green and open spaces in east and south Asia. Although we might identify variation in how these spaces are created and used they remain part of the cultural understanding of place and continue to attract significant visitor and tourist numbers.

Unfortunately, despite the positive socio-economic and ecological benefits that green infrastructure delivers in Asia there remains variability in how these resources are planned for, funded and managed. In parts of India the governance of green infrastructure is reflective of wider institutional failings to manage the landscape effectively. For example, in Ahmedabad the design of the Sabarmati Riverfront redevelopment is framed as a 10-mile greenway along the river but lacks sufficient or appropriate green infrastructure to make it more than an overheated canyon. In the planned green city of Chandigarh, in Haryana and Punjab, we see the conversion of land from green uses to spaces for housing, transport and commercial infrastructure to meet expansion needs. Even in the eco-cities of China, for example Dongtan and Tianjin, we can identify variation between what green infrastructure was proposed in the design stages (for example city parks, sustainable drainage, accessible community green space in all housing developments) and what has been delivered: large areas of mono-functional grass. It seems pertinent that the ongoing promotion of environmentally sensitive development is frequently rebranded in China to avoid acknowledging the failure of previous programmes or to promote a more contemporary form of investment. These rebrandings have included the use of terms such as 'garden', 'eco', 'sponge' and now 'forest city'. Thus, we can identify both good and bad practice in India and China, where the significant social and ecological benefits of green infrastructure are often undermined by economic or political imperatives.

In contrast, Seoul in South Korea has used a strong governance framework to convert former transport infrastructure into urban green spaces. The redevelopment of an expressway into the Cheonggyecheon Restoration Project, which transformed the site into a riverfront park, highlights what can be achieved when environmental principles are supported politically and economically. Seoul is also currently investing in the Seoullo 7017, a project that aims to redevelop a disused motorway into an elevated urban greenway. Both projects are supported by public-private partnerships but highlight how green infrastructure can be implemented in densely populated urban areas.

Case Study

Suzhou – classical and contemporary green infrastructure investment

The classic gardens of Suzhou were designated World Heritage Sites by UNESCO in 1997 due to their representation of the height of garden design in China, and remain major tourist attractions drawing people from all over China. Within Suzhou they also act as a critical reminder of the ways in which gardens can be understood as a legacy of urban development in China, and their role in linking art and literature in the understanding of the wider environment. The classical structure of the Humble Administrator's and Lion's Grove gardens uses the materials of rock, water and flora, alongside variation in height and building structure, to illustrate the complexity of human interactions with nature and the aesthetic quality of the natural environment. In addition, Suzhou and the wider Jiangsu Province are linked via canals to lakes, promoting the cultural use and appreciation of blue infrastructure within city planning. The older parts of Suzhou are also populated with smaller parks and squares, which are used by different communities simultaneously to promote various communal activities including sports, singing and dancing. In contrast to the structured and classical nature of green space in the older parts of the city, the more contemporary Singapore Industrial Park (SIP) to the east of Dushu Lake employs a European style of landscape architecture. The area is based on a grid system of tree-lined boulevards with public plazas reminiscent of North America,

→
Lion's Grove
Garden, Suzhou,
China.

↑→
Singapore
Industrial
Estate, Suzhou,
China.

which link the institutional buildings of the area. It also
has extensive grassed areas, which could be considered
mono-functional, especially as people are prohibited from using
them for recreation. These areas are subject to waterlogging
during heavy rainfall events bringing into question their
ecological value. Although SIP is aesthetically well designed
it potentially lacks the usability or ecological function needed
to support its role as a sustainable urban extension. This is
exacerbated by a lack of effective storm water management
infrastructure which leads to on-street flooding during heavy
rainfall due to an increased proportion of the area being made
of impervious surfaces, and the composition of tree planting
in some areas which does not support urban shading or the
use of outdoor spaces.

Summary

The ways in which people from different communities interact
with green infrastructure directly influence how they view the
landscapes around them. Furthermore, their experience of green
infrastructure impacts upon their current and future use of these
resources. Consequently, we see variation in how green
infrastructure is discussed, developed and valued around the
world. As stated previously this is not necessarily a bad thing, as
it offers advocates a range of options through which to invest in
landscape enhancement. However, we must be conscious that
different communities will continue to find different reasons to
use green spaces. If we can ensure that an understanding of this
process is central to the decision-making process for the
development of green infrastructure, it becomes easier to ensure
that spaces are created that are functional and appropriate for
the locations in which they are situated. This is, however, a
constantly evolving process that involves a range of stakeholders
to continually assess what they need from a landscape and what
benefits they may be able to derive from further enhancement
of the green infrastructure resource base.

Chapter 4

What Does Green Infrastructure Look Like?

This chapter discusses how we think about green infrastructure and what it looks like, with a particular focus on water and biodiversity. Water forms a key component of sustainable urban areas, and planners, architects and landscapers need to ensure that they have the right amount of water, of the right quality, in the right place within every green infrastructure project. The importance of urban nature and biodiversity is also ever more present in planning discussions, and this chapter will therefore also look at the update of nature-based planning and its role in adding ecological and economic value to urban areas.

Does all green infrastructure look the same?

There are situations where people may consider all green infrastructure to be the same – trees, grass and parks. However, unlike cities, which can be thought of as relatively homogenous in their spatial form and aesthetics, green infrastructure is more varied and dependent on its urban/rural and climatic context. Thus, we can argue that green infrastructure provides planners and developers with more options in terms of what landscape features can be incorporated into our urban areas, how these look and what benefits we can gain from them. The triptych of images on page 80 highlights this variation using Paris as an example. Paris has a history of investment in green infrastructure: parts of the city were redeveloped by Baron Haussmann between 1853–1970; there has been investment in city-scale parks (the Bois de Boulogne, Bois de Vincennes and Parc des Buttes-Chaumont, for example); and more recently there has been a

← Jardin du Luxembourg, Paris, France.

← Parc André Citroën, Paris, France.

← Promenade Plantée, Paris, France.

renewal of derelict sites into parks in demographically diverse arrondissements. The outcome of these changes is a dynamism in the city's green infrastructure that illustrates the diversity of design and the role it can play in encouraging people to use the city's green and open space.

Advocates of green infrastructure look to cities such as Paris, Vancouver and Melbourne as exemplars of how landscape diversity can be embedded within urban areas. As noted in the first chapter the breadth of what green infrastructure 'is' provides scope to think innovatively about landscape and how it can be embedded within the fabric of our cities. Moreover, the seasonal and climatic variation seen in our landscapes, especially in cities with tropical or monsoonal climates, promotes a more diverse use of species to ensure that the aesthetic and ecological functionality of a green space fits within the given location. Thus, discussions of green infrastructure need to consider both the location and climate to ensure that the most appropriate selection of biodiverse species are used. In addition, the benefits that are promoted through green infrastructure will vary depending on the location. For instance, flood mitigation or heat island amelioration may be important benefits in Canada or China respectively, and influence what green infrastructure is used. This, in turn, shapes decision-making in terms of the aesthetic and functional qualities that are promoted by investment in green infrastructure. In some locations the aesthetics may be the most prominent driver of investment, as in Paris, whilst in other areas the landscape functionality could be more pertinent, as in Wicken Fen in Cambridgeshire or the Walthamstow Wetlands in London. To get the right green infrastructure in the right place requires us to be contextually aware of the location, its existing landscape (and problems associated with it), and the desires or aspirations of that area.

—

Water – blue infrastructure management and development

Water or 'blue infrastructure' is an essential aspect of green infrastructure thinking. Whilst there is an argument that water infrastructure should be considered as being separate from terrestrial-based landscape resource management, this could be seen as undermining the consensus built around the use of green infrastructure terminology. We can also propose that integrating water management into a wider green infrastructure approach to landscape management provides a more holistic understanding of how different environmental resources interact and support each other. Thus, if water is located separately from green infrastructure discussions we may simply be reiterating historical divisions within landscape and urban planning. It also limits the inclusion of multi-disciplinary expertise into the management of environment resources.

Despite the ongoing discussion of how best to locate discussions of water within green infrastructure thinking, water has been and remains a key element in these debates. This reflects not only the ways in which water has shaped the form of urban environments but also the inherent costs associated with engineering the management of water in such locations. For many cities water has historically been seen as an essential resource but a costly one that they have tried to manage through engineered solutions. Within green infrastructure planning water is viewed as an evolving resource that should be worked with rather than controlled. Thus, engineered solutions such as the channelisation of the River Don in Sheffield, England, or the Los Angeles River in Los Angeles are viewed as examples where controlling the watercourse has led to greater complexity in water management. Using a green infrastructure approach to water management can deliver a series of options whereby the scale, location and flow of a watercourse can be adapted through more NBSs to improve the sustainability of the resource, such as the improvements seen on the Emscher River within the VALUE project. This can be done through the development of localised investments in water-sensitive design such as bioswales or rain gardens to larger SuDS. Each has benefits in terms of managing water resources and can form part of a wider water-sensitive network of green infrastructure resources. Key to this is an understanding of:

- The connective nature of water within and across urban areas,
- The dynamics of a watercourse and the seasonal changes associated with rainfall and periods of drought,
- The costs of green infrastructure as a form of management compared to engineered solutions,
- The scale and appropriateness of water sensitive design and the use of SuDS and household water management systems.

An understanding of connectivity within water management provides a spatial outline of where these resources can be found, how big they are and what benefits they can deliver. Shanghai is an example of a city where a network of blue infrastructure, here including the Huangpu River and Suzhou Creek, is linked to the wider management of the city's water resources. Ahmedabad in India is another example; its main water body, the Sabarmati River, is utilised to support the management of the city's lake system by managing its flow and discharge. The water network of London can also be seen to centre on the management of the River Thames by Thames Water and other public and private institutions. This includes an understanding of how the tributaries of the Thames are managed and has seen an increased investment in SuDS in the Queen Elizabeth Olympic Park in Stratford and in Mayesbrook Park in Barking and Dagenham. Thames Water are also working with BIDs along the Thames in the Team London Bridge area to ensure that surface water runoff can be managed through an increased use of rain gardens and other SuDS.

Potentially the most prominent SuDS project that employs an understanding of water connectivity is the Emerald Necklace in Boston. Covering an area of approximately 450 hectares of linked parks, waterways and parkways, and designed by Frederick Law Olmsted, the Emerald Necklace was constructed to mitigate the impacts of seasonal flooding of homes, businesses and transport routes in the city of Boston and the town of Brookline. Since its development the project has diversified to include flora and fauna that are more responsive to the area's weather, for example on the Mother's Rest area of the Back Bay Fens and the Spring Pond Wildflower Meadow in Olmsted Park. It has also made use of wetland areas in the Back Bay area to ensure that seasonal fluctuations in flow do not adversely impact on the surrounding homes or businesses.

The responsiveness of the Emerald Necklace to fluctuations in seasonal rainfall (and snowmelt) has been described as a key benefit of using SuDS in urban development. Chicago has seen investment in bioswales to help mitigate the peak flow of spring snowmelt and rainfall, with the aim of reducing surface water flooding. In New Delhi, such practices are known but not always followed: the redevelopment of the Yamuna riverfront has led to rising concerns over the sustainability of building on the floodplain. As in many cities New Delhi's government has identified the riverfront as a prime location for real-estate speculation. However, by removing the area's vegetation they have substantially modified the floodplain ecosystem leading to an increased likelihood of seasonal flood events taking place. Other cities have taken notice of such developments and attempted to work with their water resources to manage seasonal changes. For example, in China we are seeing a growing discussion of 'sponge cities' as a way to address extreme weather events. Launched in 2015, 16 cities including Lingang and Xiamen have started to plan for the use of green infrastructure to address urban water management issues by using porous pavements, bioswales, green roofs and retention ponds as methods of stabilising water fluctuation in urban systems. Although sponge city thinking remains in its infancy China is drawing on the vast evidence base of SuDS research, especially that developed in the USA, to illustrate how NBSs can be as effective as engineered solutions.

A key aspect of the sponge city discussion has been that investing in green infrastructure costs less than engineered solutions. Due to the variability of options considered as SuDS and the associated knowledge needed to install and manage them, it can seem that investment in water sensitive design is uneconomical. However, creating SuDS can be as simple or as complicated as the location (or building) requires. At their most basic SuDS can be man-made (but green) channels cut into a landscape to receive excess rainfall or overflow. This can be scaled up to more complex systems where bioswales (wide ditches/channels with sloping sides filled with plants or riprap), retention ponds (artificial lakes/ponds/pools used to hold water and release it at later time), porous pavements or surfaces, and green walls and roofs are utilised to manage an urban-scale water system. As more elements are added into this process the cost of design, implementation and maintenance increases. However, recent experiences in Cambourne in Cambridgeshire, the Greenwich Millennium Village and the Victoria BID green roof project in London have shown that with technical knowledge effective investment in SuDS can take place. It is therefore crucial to identify what the most appropriate SuDS intervention is for a given location and budget, as poorly executed green walls or roofs can die relatively quickly. Consequently, there remains concern that water sensitive green infrastructure investment will be less effective than engineered solutions, with many engineers continuing to question the viability of green infrastructure due to the costs of retrofitting buildings and ongoing maintenance. They also query the effectiveness of environmental systems, which can be modelled but are not as predictable as other forms of water management. This view is particularly prevalent where the failure of an investment, for example the Los Angeles River flood control channel, would have major consequences for urban populations. Recent research, however, has argued that a re-naturing of the Los Angeles River is a more cost-effective way of managing excess runoff than continuing to invest in maintaining the concrete channel. Moreover, the PlaNYC stated that investment in green infrastructure would decrease the costs of combined sewer overflows by over US$1 billion compared to developing built infrastructure. It also stated that although the payback time for an investment would be longer than with conventional engineered solutions it could lead to greater savings and increased returns compared to grey infrastructure.

Case Study

Chicago — managing the city's water

Chicago is a city that suffers annual surface water flooding, with the associated damage caused to homes, and has worked extensively with water sensitive design and SuDS to mitigate

↑ →
Commercial
building,
International
Corporate
Headquarters
Hoffmann
Estates, Illinois,
USA.

these issues at a city and local level. As has been discussed, the
Chicago River has been re-engineered by the city, the MWRD
and the US Army Corps to ensure it flows away from Lake
Michigan into specifically created 'forest preserve wetlands'
(i.e. wetlands within forest preserves) as part of their forest
preserve sites that promote seasonal flooding. Chicago has also
looked at ways to integrate more effective control of its water
resources through the management of parks, which have
included improving the connectivity of linear greenways and
water bodies. In addition, the city has promoted the inclusion
of SuDS in new urban development to limit localised on-street
flooding, for example in South Chicago where schools, public
buildings and new homes are being fitted with bioswales and
rain gardens. Although these are small interventions, the

→
Rain gardens,
Advocate
Lutheran
General Hospital,
Patient Tower,
Illinois, USA.

growing number of such investments has led to a significant
cumulative positive impact being identified for storm water
management. There is also a growing understanding, promoted
by organisations such as the Center for Neighborhood
Technology (CNT), that individuals can be more actively
engaged in storm water protection at a household level. They
have invested in a series of programmes that educate people in
how to integrate rain gardens onto their property, as well as the
use of rain barrels and other small-scale interventions to lower
on-site and on-street surface water runoff. The CNT also offers
loans to homeowners to buy the materials to implement SuDS
projects. This multi-level approach has placed Chicago,
alongside cities such as New York and Philadelphia, at the
forefront of SuDS and water management in the USA.

—

Street trees, urban woodlands and community forestry

The use of street trees, woodlands and community forestry is a
popular and successful way to integrate green infrastructure into
urban areas. Due to the versatility of planting techniques, trees
can be integrated into ecologically marginal areas, as well as
high-density urban areas. Thus, they provide opportunities across
a range of urban and socio-economic landscapes to invest in
green infrastructure. Moreover, if we start to break down the

composition of green infrastructure in urban areas we can identify that a significant proportion comprises trees or woodland. Examples include the urban forests or *bois* of Paris or the Parco Sud and Nord of Milan. In Singapore the 2013 Land Use Plan called for all citizens to live within 400 metres of a tree. The Massachusetts Institute of Technology (MIT) and the World Economic Forum developed the 'Treepedia' analysis tool to illustrate the spatial extent of tree coverage in a number of cities. From their analysis they argued that approximately 25.9 per cent of Vancouver's land cover is made up of tree canopy. They highlight that Geneva in Switzerland, Vienna in Austria and Johannesburg in South Africa also benefit extensively both ecologically and socio-ecologically from having significant urban woodlands (see http://senseable.mit.edu/treepedia). Although the canopy cover of each of these cities is a key variable in the Treepedia scoring we need to look further at the social, economic and ecological benefits that they provide to identify why street trees, woodland and urban forestry are key forms of green infrastructure investment.

In the UK, urban woodlands and community forestry have been promoted by the Forestry Commission, Natural England and England's Community Forest partnerships as a means of rehabilitating post-industrial landscapes. Across England we have seen former industrial sites, many of which are considered exclusionary and dangerous by communities, being transformed through investment in green infrastructure into high-quality green spaces. This includes the provision of new woodlands in the urban fringe of England's main urban areas as a way of increasing their functionality. In addition, they provide important elements in the wider urban/rural mosaics by creating new habitats for birds, amphibians and animals. Locations around Manchester, Liverpool and Newcastle have seen significant investment in community forestry coordinated by England's Community Forests. The benefits of these projects have included greater engagement by communities with the landscapes, increased environmental awareness through forest and church school projects, and changes in sporting and recreational behaviour associated with landscape enhancement. The current discussion regarding a 'Northern Forest', associated with the Department for Environment, Food and Rural Affairs (DEFRA) 25 Year Environment Plan (2018), highlights the UK government's proposals to invest in forestry at a national scale. The project aims to plant over 50 million trees across the M62 transport corridor between Liverpool and Hull to deliver a variety of health, well-being, real-estate and biodiversity benefits to the UK economy. In addition, the project will help mitigate flooding from extreme weather events and help tackle air pollution associated with increased congestion on the M62. Although the UK government has only committed £5.7 million to the project there is an expectation that its visibility and geographical breadth will attract investment from other commercial and industrial backers. Although this suggests that national-level investment in green infrastructure can be achieved, we have seen more frequent development of such projects at a city or local scale.

In New York, the Million Trees NYC programme attracted a high level of engagement from local communities who helped plant the trees and thereafter monitor the investment. The project was also used to educate communities about the added ecological value that trees have in urban areas. This included the discussion of habitat creation, more effective storm water management and improved aesthetic values. The Trees for Cities project in London approaches investment in urban forestry in a similar way. Working with local government, community groups and the commercial sector, they have engaged over 70,000 people since 1993 and planted over 600,000 trees in parks, schools (through edible playgrounds), housing estates and public areas. Their aim is to plant over a million trees in London to help mitigate the impacts of land conversion and development (including increased CO_2, construction dust and other noxious gases) and improve the liveability of the city. The use of community-led approaches is key to the work of Trees for Cities, as they view woodlands as places for people. Thus, by working with communities to design and plant trees in urban areas of London, Bradford and Birmingham they aim to generate a long-term investment in their management by local people.

→
Street trees in
New Delhi, India.

→
Lodi Gardens,
New Delhi, India.

Case Study

New Delhi – mitigating development and informal use of green infrastructure

New Delhi is a constantly changing city. With an annual growth rate of approximately 5 per cent, pressures on its landscape are continually increasing. However, New Delhi can be considered as one of the greenest cities in India with areas to the south, east and west rich in green and blue spaces linked to its colonial expansion. These include the New Delhi Green Belt (the Delhi Ridge), the Secretariat and River Yamuna catchment, in addition to biodiversity parks in the south of the city. In total, this equates to approximately 22 per cent of the land area or 15 square metres of green space per person (compared to 0.88 square metres in Mumbai and 6.4 square metres in Bengaluru). Tree cover forms almost 43 square miles of this figure, whilst forests cover over 73 square miles. However, the most effective form of green infrastructure is its street trees. These are ubiquitous across the city, being used to line roads, residential areas and public areas. They provide locations for business with many independent and informal activities taking place underneath trees. Around road junctions, transport hubs and tourist attractions, businesses thrive under the available tree canopy. They are key habitats for the city's bird and animal life and provide much-needed canopy cover during monsoon rain events. The latter is especially important as the water and sewage systems of New Delhi are over-subscribed and excess rainfall can lead to surface water flooding, increased water pollution and the spread of some communicable diseases. In addition, *The Times of India* reported that the NGO Delhi Greens stated that each healthy tree contributes Rs 23.72 lakhs (approximately £26,000) per annum in oxygen production and air pollution mitigation to the city's economy. Although trees are recognised as providing important socio-economic and ecological functions, the pace of development in New Delhi, and particularly in the National Capital Territory (NCT), is placing increasing pressures on the retention of these resources. Consequently, Greenpeace India and the Environment Ministry have worked with communities, the city government and developers to educate them into more effective forms of land use development. This has included issuing fines for polluting activities and promoting the increased use of trees to moderate the spread of dust and flooding.

Case Study

Landscape reclamation and rejuvenation using green infrastructure in northern England

Street trees and community forests have been used across the north of England to aid the regeneration of areas that have suffered post-industrial decline. Around Sunderland and County Durham the former coal mining sites in Penshaw and Hetton-le-Hole have received funding from England's Community Forests, local government and environmental organisations to help rehabilitate derelict spaces. In Hetton Lyons Country Park in Hetton-le-Hole the North-East

↑ →
Street green
infrastructure,
Salford, UK.

Community Forest Partnership was involved in the creation
of a new park with facilities to accommodate outdoor activities
such as cycling, fishing and football. These were blended with
a diverse ecological environment associated with the country
park's lake making it an important habitat for birds and insects.
Also in the north-east West Park in Darlington was designed to
act as a sustainable community hub and integrates a 12-hectare
nature reserve into its 49-hectare housing site. The park is seen
as a key local biodiversity resource providing a habitat for water
voles, dingy skipper butterflies and ringed plover birds, and is a
designated local nature reserve. The site also employs a levy to

help the park, as all residents in the West Park development pay a charge to cover the costs of managing the site. In Manchester and Salford, the Red Rose Forest, now Manchester City of Trees, has worked extensively to increase the proportion of street trees across Greater Manchester. To date they have planted over 250,000 trees, improved 223 hectares of heritage woodland and helped over 10,000 people engage with the natural landscape. This has been achieved through the planting and managing of woodlands in marginal urban areas to develop an added socio-economic and ecological value in those places. They have also engaged with schools through tree planting projects and educational programmes, as well as working with developers to deliver their 'green streets' mandate of investing in green infrastructure in housing developments. In addition, Manchester City of Trees has worked with Manchester City Council, local environmental organisations and the city's universities to establish the added economic value that investment in street trees can deliver. This research was reported in VALUE, where a city-scale tree planting programme could see significant returns in terms of increased business rates and council tax on residential property. We can also identify similar levels of investment and landscape enhancement work in the Merseyside and Cheshire where the Mersey Forest has led a series of projects including Forest Schools and 'Natural Health Service' programmes that have made significant use of the tree planting to raise awareness of the social and health value of green infrastructure. More widely the Mersey Forest has been a leading force promoting the role that street trees can play in meeting both the climatic and socio-economic needs of urban areas in the north-west of England.

—

The use of green infrastructure to mitigate climatic variation
In locations which experience extreme temperature, wind or rainfall there is a growing evidence base that green infrastructure can be used to effectively mitigate the impacts of climate change. This can include smaller interventions in street trees and roadside greening to intercept pollution and rainfall as well as city-scale SuDS systems that help mitigate urban heat island at a landscape scale. Cities in the Mediterranean, such as Bari in Italy, are investing in urban greening as a cooling mechanism. In the megacities of Asia there is a growing awareness of the value of

green spaces as 'urban cooling systems' that help to address the effects of heat and humidity. The key value in urban climate management of green infrastructure is therefore the variety of options available to planners and landscape professionals.

However, the development of green infrastructure is not a guarantee that extreme climate variation can be controlled. Again, we must consider each location as being specific in terms of its physical geography, its urban form and its socio-cultural needs. Thus, actions that would help mitigate urban heat island issues in Europe may not be as successful on the Indian sub-continent. Where we do see green infrastructure making a positive contribution to urban climate management, it is because a more holistic approach to development is taken. For example, Singapore is repeatedly reported as being a world leader in the use of urban greening to mitigate its heat and humidity. In 2010 approximately 8 per cent of the country's land cover was classified as parks and nature reserves. The Sustainable Singapore Blueprint calls for an increase in green infrastructure to 10 per cent by 2030, a target supported by the Inter-Ministerial Committee on Sustainable Development (IMCSD), co-chaired by the Minister for National Development and the Minister for the Environment and Water Resources. Although this is smaller than other cities, the 8 per cent comprises three large nature reserves which act as the 'lungs' of the city. They help to intercept and hold rainfall in the monsoon and provide a resource that cools the city during the summer. In addition, to address the problem of surface water flooding, the city has built upon the 1972 Water Master Plan and invested extensively in green infrastructure in the form of green roofs, porous pavements and SuDS to lower the impact of peak flow flood events. This has aided the city in managing its water resource base in terms of quality and quantity, and it has lowered the economic impact of disruption associated with extreme weather events.

A comparable set of approaches to Singapore's use of nature reserves as green lungs can be seen in European cities. In Paris, the urban forests of the Bois de Boulogne (2100 acres) and Bois de Vincennes (2450 acres) are proposed as city-scale resources that moderate the city's temperature in the summer months, intercept extensive rainfall (which is used to fill lakes in the Bois), and provide extensive recreational opportunities close to the city. When viewed as part of the wider Parisian green network that extends out into the Ile-de-France, the Bois act as biodiverse and water sensitive green infrastructure hubs. Stuttgart is a further example of how urban green infrastructure can mitigate climatic variation, where the growth of transport infrastructure and housing has led to an increased densification and 'greying' of the city. This saw the conversion of green spaces into built infrastructure, which has had an impact on the city's climate, especially in terms of prevailing winds and a growing urban heat island effect. To address this issue the regional and city governments have worked with landscape and built environment professionals to integrate a greater proportion of green infrastructure along key arterial routes across the city. Through their Landschaftpark project they have invested over €15 million in 120 projects to improve the resilience of the city's landscape to climate change. Consequently, as of 2007, approximately 60 per cent of the city is now considered to be 'green'. This includes: 5000 hectares of forest and woodland, 65,000 trees in parks and open spaces, 35,000 street trees, 300,000 square metres of green rooftops, and out of 155 miles of tram tracks, 25 miles have been grassed. This has allowed the city's streets to intercept pollutants caused by traffic and consequently develop a city-wide mosaic of green spaces providing additional habitats and respite from heat stress, and to mitigate the impacts of peak rainfall events.

European cities, as discussed by Beatley (see *Green Urbanism: Learning from European Cities* (2000) for further examples), have been seen to be leading the field in climate change adaptation. However, there is a growing evidence base focussing on Asia and South American cities revealing active engagement in climate change adaptation. In some cases, this is a direct response to the physical precariousness of a location, such as flood mitigation in Dhaka through increased tree planting. Elsewhere it is a response to concerns over the capacity of the natural environment to support continued industrial growth and the associated transport and housing requirements, such as is witnessed in ongoing issues of landscape protection in Chinese cities. In such locations, tensions exist between the acknowledgement of the problems associated with climate change, especially for lower income populations, and the need to meet growth targets. One example of this dilemma is Chandigarh in north-west India. Developed as planned green city post-independence from the British in 1947, Chandigarh integrated green infrastructure into the DNA of its city plan. Designed as a modular city with each sector having housing, commercial spaces and parks, green corridors or water bodies, Chandigarh ensured that all residents would have access to green infrastructure. However, as the city has expanded to house over a million people, pressures have been placed on its green spaces, which are being converted into built infrastructure. One consequence of this is an increase in heat stress events, which would previously have been mitigated through the evapotranspiration properties of urban street trees. In addition, there is an increased need for water which is impacting on the sustainability of the green infrastructure resource base and the health of the Sukhna Lake. Chandigarh is not unusual in its development context. Locations such as Dwarka and Gurgaon in the National Capital Territory (NCT) of New Delhi are engaged in similar debates regarding the ways in which the landscape can help mitigate the impacts of industrial pollution, especially construction dust and water shortages.

One success story has been in Bengaluru where the functional and reputational damage caused by a 50-year period of growth impacted on its 'garden city' status. As the city grew to over 12 million people, the rate of land conversion from urban forests and water bodies into grey infrastructure outstripped the ability of the environment to function effectively. The result was an increased incidence of urban flooding due to a lack of natural or permeable surfaces and a corresponding rise in citywide temperatures. Kumar, Geneletti and Nagendra (2016) calculated that this expansion meant that 91 per cent of the city's total area was vulnerable to changing climatic conditions. To mitigate these issues the city's government has diverted a significant proportion of urban development funding to re-invest in urban street trees and street-side greening to enhance the quality and environmental function of the city's main parks, and to improve the connectivity of its water bodies. The city's government has also been more selective in its choice of plant species to increase the level of resilience to water and heat stress. Additional funding for green infrastructure has also been collected through housing taxes, development levies and road traffic fines. The outcome has been a decrease in the level of flooding and a moderation of the average temperature across the city.

___

Case Study

Darjeeling – using urban greening to limit the impacts of climate change

Located in an upland region of West Bengal in north-east India, Darjeeling is a town that is known for its agricultural products, most famously tea, but also for its marginal environmental capacity. Due to its temperate climate, it became the location of the British colonial administration in the summer months and grew in size as a consequence. However, the steep slopes of the region and the lack of flat land have meant that development has modified the soil and ecological structure of the area. Over time this has led to increased landslides, surface water flooding and a growing marginality of available potable water due to overuse by tea farmers. In response, a number of charities and NGOs have worked with local communities, businesses and the local government to propose investment in trees and shrubs and a rethinking of the clearing of woodlands to help stabilise the area's slopes. This has been met with some success as some larger landowners have been able to see the long-term benefits of using green infrastructure to maintain the ecological capacity of the area. However, farmers with more marginal tenure have been less forthcoming in their adoption of tree planting and water management practices. The local government of Darjeeling is aware of the value of investing in urban woodlands as a mechanism to stop landslides and is therefore engaged in discussions to increase the woodland cover on the slopes surrounding the town. They have also been in a dialogue with the Indian Army Engineers to ensure that new water facilities are more responsive to the changing climate and ecological structure of the upland landscape. Again, this has led to some successes over the ways in which water is extracted yet there remains reluctance in some quarters to move away from established engineered practices.

↑ →
Urban greening,
Darjeeling, India.

Consequently, although Darjeeling's use of green infrastructure
is increasing, the area remains precariously balanced
environmentally as it tries to provide sufficient socio-economic
opportunities for its population whilst ensuring that its
landscape remains functional.

Innovation in green infrastructure

Innovation in green infrastructure can take many forms. It can
be implemented and function at several scales, and importantly
it can deliver a variety of benefits to different groups of people.
This includes adapting built infrastructure to changing climatic
conditions such as increased heat, wind or rain through the
provision of green walls and roofs in central London. It can

mean more attention being paid to the development of inclusive play equipment, benches and rubbish bins in pocket parks to encourage families and older people to use these sites in Manhattan. It can mean the retrofitting of sustainable drainage systems in homes prone to flooding in Chicago or the creation of edible gardens in school to provide students with access to fresh fruit and vegetables in Berkeley, California. Each of these ideas is relatively small scale in nature, but we can also identify large-scale projects such as the creation and enhancement of wetlands in Chicago or the use of SuDS and inclusive play and green spaces in the developing Thamesmead master plan being developed by the Peabody Trust in Greater London. Innovation, therefore, does not necessarily mean novel or new forms of technology, although the green roof research in Barking Riverside being developed by the University of East London is looking at alternative seed, structure and technology mixes to address changing climatic conditions. Alternatively, innovation can focus on changing the physical or psychological role that green infrastructure plays in how we interact with and value the landscapes around us. Assessing green infrastructure through this perspective we can identify a much wider range of projects, many of which have already been discussed, that are making a more effective use of the landscape resource base in our urban areas.

Although new technology is not vital for innovation it should be considered as part of the conversation. For example, in the Adlershof district of Berlin a new City of Science, Technology and Media is being developed, which makes use of existing and more innovative types of green infrastructure. The area integrates a series of SuDS via street swales that are effective during heavy rainfall. These are complemented by permeable plastic 'paving grids' that are placed on grass to provide additional support for emergency services who have to access the area when it is waterlogged. Also in Berlin, a range of retention ponds, bioswales, rain gardens and rain chains have been used in the Rummelsburg development to provide greater control over the level of surface water flooding in the area. The landscape architects of the project also planned in parkscapes (Medaillonplatz), a riverfront promenade (Liegewiese An Der Rummelsburger Bucht) and adventure play spaces to make the area as attractive as possible for the local communities. These examples illustrate how seemingly small interventions can create a cumulatively greater benefit for an area by using a variety of green infrastructure options.

The Glasgow and Clyde Valley (GCV) Green Network Vision is a further example where a variety of approaches have been taken to improve the ecological and social value of the landscape. The vision aims to rehabilitate over 14 square miles of vacant or derelict space through the provision of new and improved urban green infrastructure in the form of street trees, green walls and roofs and rain gardens, 4000 community growing spaces, 195 square miles of new wildlife habitat and 620 miles of active travel routes. Through the use of a range of green infrastructure options, the GCV Green Network Partnership aims to facilitate a change in policy-maker thinking and the behaviour of people in the area who will have greater access to green and open space in the Clyde Valley area. This is of particular importance to the health of local people who are considered in many studies to be significantly at risk of ill health due to a lack of access and interaction with outdoor landscapes.

The development of the Connswater Greenway in Belfast also highlights comparable uses of different forms of green infrastructure to ensure that the physical landscape is functional for local people, and that it provides a resilient landscape to changing weather events. The creation of a wetland in Orangefield Park enables the Knock River to flood periodically in a controlled manner meaning less disruption to local homes. In addition, areas of the river course have been de-culverted to provide access to the channel and to allow a greater range of biodiversity to colonise the area. Along the length of the Connswater Greenway there have also been investments in tree planting and the creation of wildflower meadows to provide additional diversity to the ecological profile of the site. Comparisons can be made to the development of the Queen Elizabeth Olympic Park where the creation of a floodable wetland on the River Lea is protecting over 5000 homes from flooding.

London – innovative green infrastructure investment

Greater London is currently engaging in a series of projects that illustrate the ways in which green infrastructure can be used to meet changing social, ecological and economic needs. The highest-profile project is the transformation of a 1-square-mile area of industrial land in Stratford into the Queen Elizabeth Olympic Park, but there are many other developments that could be considered to be equally innovative. The redevelopment of Kings Place in central London from former railyard infrastructure into a new campus for the University of the Arts with 200 metres of green wall and a green roof garden is one such example. The site is also creating a 'skip garden' to encourage urban gardening, as well as the development of the 8094-square-metre Camley Street Natural Park run by the London Wildlife Trust. Overall 40 per

↑→
Greening the
grey, London.

cent of the 67-acre site is green space. There is further reuse of railway infrastructure planned in the Camden Highline proposals, which aim to repurpose derelict and underused transport infrastructure between Camden and King's Cross to increase connectivity and access to nature. Although the project remains in its infancy many commentators view it as potentially being a significant investment in urban greening. Moreover, in the Bankside area of south London investments are being made in street-scale green infrastructure interventions through the implementation of community gardens and areas for food growing. The Better Bankside BID has worked with Transport for London (TfL), local schools and Southwark Council to use urban greening as a traffic calming measure. This has been achieved by changing the street layout, removing parking and increasing the level of greening along the street. Each of these projects has used green infrastructure as a mechanism to improve the visibility, accessibility and functionality of the urban environment. This helped the development of a campaign to name London a 'National Park City'. The roots of this campaign emerged as a need to promote the green infrastructure of London as a critical and high-quality resource base. Although the London National Park City may not have legal authority to develop green infrastructure it has raised the visibility of urban greening as a key factor in promoting urban liveability, and is being used by the Mayor of London to drive forward a strong environmental agenda within the developing London Plan.

Case Study

Bosco Verticale — a forest in the sky

Located in the Porta Nuova district of Milan between the Via Gaetano de Castillia and Via Federico Confalonieri, near Milano Porta Garibaldi railway station, the Bosco Verticale (completed in 2014) comprises two tower blocks, which house over 900 trees on 8900 square metres of apartment terraces. In Boeri Studio's design, the use of trees in apartment towers was seen as a way of mitigating smog and filtering fine particulate matter from the atmosphere in central Milan. It provides a large-scale green infrastructure resource and is highly visible but located on a small spatial footprint. In addition to the trees, the development utilises over 5000 shrubs and 11,000 perennials to shroud the tower blocks in a green facade. Additional benefits identified for the development include the absorption of CO_2 and the production of oxygen. The trees also act to protect the building against radiation and noise pollution thus reducing heating and cooling costs.

↑→
Bosco Verticale,
Milan, Italy.

Summary

Green infrastructure can take a variety of forms, provide a range of functions and address a multitude of socio-economic and ecological issues within and across urban areas. Consequently, we cannot identify a singular approach to green infrastructure investment that works in all locations. Each project, neighbourhood or city needs to take stock of what green infrastructure it has, what it wants to improve on and how much funding is available. The improvement needed can take the form of investments in street greening, trees and woodlands, SuDS or more innovative uses of green space. All have their values and drawbacks but provide a suite of options that planners, landscape architects, communities and city decision-makers can use to find the most appropriate form of investment. Moreover, as city planners become increasingly aware of the impacts of continued urbanisation on climate change, water management and biodiversity we are starting to see a coalescence of understanding within planning that the use of NBSs can have a positive impact on these changes. Likewise, as the understanding of the costs, management and long-term benefits of investment in green infrastructure become known (or better evidenced) we are starting to see a growing uptake of its principles within development. This is seen throughout Europe and North America and increasingly in South America, Asia and significantly in African countries where the pressures of urbanisation and environmental capacity are potentially most acute. What is clear is that an acceptance of green infrastructure as a multifaceted approach to planning, which integrates knowledge of urban, economic and environmental systems into decision-making, can make its use more effective and contextually appropriate.

Bigger, Bolder and Better: Innovation in Green Infrastructure Practice

This chapter reflects upon how green infrastructure is being used around the world to promote innovation in urban and landscape design. This focusses on the ways in which it is being used in post-industrial cities in Europe to reconsider how we value derelict sites, how it can meet changing urban planning needs around the world, especially in rapidly developing Asian cities, and how green infrastructure is being employed by planners and developers to rethink the relationship people have with the landscapes around them. The key message of this chapter are that green infrastructure can be used to address pre-existing landscape issues, such as dereliction associated with urban change, as well as to think more boldly about how cities can use their environmental resources to create multi-functional landscapes. Where this is achievable, for example in the Ruhr in Germany or Atlanta in the USA, we can identify a growing association between green infrastructure, urban renewal and socio-economic prosperity.

How do we make better green infrastructure?
Applying value to green infrastructure, as discussed in Chapter 3, is a subjective process. Individually, and as communities, we all identify with different aspects of the landscape that we consider to be important elements supporting our socio-economic interaction. Consequently, when landscape architects are designing spaces they are often attempting to provide amenity, aesthetic and ecological diversity to meet the broad-ranging needs of society. They are also aiming to meet the economic

needs of development by creating places that people want to live or spend time in. However, if we focus on how the core principles of green infrastructure outlined in Chapter 1 are integrated into a design, a development or a location, we can start to identify how we create more inclusive, sustainable and interactive spaces. To ensure that this is achieved we need to consider a number of key issues, including:

- the scale of a development and its interaction with the wider environment,
- the creation and maintenance of diversity in the visual and interactive nature of a site,
- an understanding of how green infrastructure can be integrated into the lives of people thus becoming accessible, connected and functional, and
- planning for an evolving landscape in terms of its ecology and value to its users.

By reflecting on each of these issues we can identify projects that have successfully navigated the design, provision and management of investment in green infrastructure. However, we should not assess each in isolation, as people's engagement with landscape is shaped by the ways in which it provides a range of amenities (physical, psychological and visual) for different members of a community. Reviewing green infrastructure development in terms of its scale, aesthetics, functions and socio-economic/ecological value therefore provides a basis to assess its likelihood of being considered valuable.

For example, the scale of an investment is important, as it has to be reflective of the space available, the activities that are being planned for a site and how many people are expected to use it. In large city parks such as Central Park in New York or the People's Park in Shanghai the scale of the site provides opportunities for a multitude of activities to take place simultaneously. Consequently, there is scope within the design to provide for a variety of landscapes within each park, ensuring that there is 'something for everyone'. This may include grassed areas but also play and sports provision, wildlife areas, water features and walking/cycling infrastructure. However, such diversity may not be appropriate for smaller sites such as pocket parks. Again in New York, we see the value of smaller and less diverse spaces; localised community amenities that are used by families in adjacent apartments. In Liverpool we can identify a similar situation where the city's major parks, Calderstones, Sefton and Newsham, attract visitors from all over the city as they provide a range of recreational, social and ecological functions. We also see, though, a significant use of local parks and green spaces at a neighbourhood scale which are more easily accessible and can be used for dog walking, jogging or play. In such cases the size of the space is appropriate to the locality and its use as an everyday space. Across the world we see similar hierarchies of green infrastructure where city-scale spaces provide more functions but are not necessarily the spaces that people use most frequently. Thus, there is a need to reflect on community provision that fits within local contexts to ensure a range of green infrastructure resources is available.

In addition to scale, green infrastructure planning requires an understanding of the links between functions, amenities and aesthetics. Where all three elements can be effectively integrated we see spaces that are valued and used. However, where they are not in sync spaces can become marginalised or isolationist. We therefore need to reflect on what we are developing, where and for whom to ensure that an investment is appropriate. This can be achieved through effective consultation and collaboration between landscape and planning professionals, the development and environment sectors, and the public. The latter are especially important, as they are the people who will use these spaces most frequently, and are the arbitrators of whether a space works. Thus by understanding the needs of different communities, such as older people, young families or immigrants, we can start to identify what activities or features are most appropriate (cf. CABE Space, 2005; 2009). This may be as simple as providing benches around a location for people to sit on, having a variety of sports or recreational facilities, or making the site accessible to people with mobility issues. Victoria Park in Belfast is an example of a green infrastructure site that has attempted to integrate a variety of amenities and functions within its boundaries to encourage different groups to use it. This is supported by better access, parking, toilet and refreshment facilities that have helped to make the park more attractive and comfortable. Victoria Park is also managed to ensure that the Victorian layout is maintained. Such a level of park management is costly but is viewed by many as being an important factor influencing their use of a space, as it is deemed to be safer. Thus, the aesthetic quality of a space is linked to use and a perception of whether a green infrastructure resource is cared for and managed effectively.

Where parks and green spaces are managed effectively and are attractive they can become well patronised. Such spaces can also be increasingly diverse in their spatial form, as people may be willing to accept some forms of evolution in a site's composition. One example is Heaton Park in north Manchester, which has invested in a treetop trekking facility that allows people to use ropes and boardwalks to walk at a 15-metre height in the park's trees. This investment has meant that a section of the park is now privatised but it is seen by visitors as offering something new for its users (although there is a fee charged for its use). Likewise, the development of the Gardens by the Bay in Singapore has created a 101-hectare privately owned space that is a major attraction for people visiting the city. Although most noticeable for the visually stunning 'Supertree Grove', the site also provides recreational spaces and educational opportunities to learn about climate change and environmental management. By developing a bigger, bolder and more striking location that integrates landscape design, functionality and accessibility the site has become an essential attraction for Singapore's visitors and and residents.

Where the Gardens by the Bay and Heaton Park have prospered has been in their understanding of the variety of activities that people visiting a green infrastructure site want to engage with. They are purposefully multi-functional in terms of providing key climatic and water system management activities, whilst also ensuring that socio-economic amenities are available for patrons. Thus, by reflecting on what a site will be used for, for example early morning yoga, walking and social interaction in Parimal Garden, Ahmedabad, or weddings at 'marriage corner' in

Shanghai's People's Park, we can start to appreciate how green infrastructure can be integrated into people's everyday lives. Such a discussion also touches on the ways in which we understand the evolution of a landscape. In a large proportion of European and North American parks the changing seasons bring with them a change in the flora and fauna, temperature and uses of a site. Landscape architects work with nature to ensure that green infrastructure remains functional throughout the year. This means the use of a range of flora and fauna that is both appropriate to the climate, for example the plants used on the High Line in New York, and reactive to changing levels of use and need, e.g. the density and types of planting used in the Queen Elizabeth Olympic Park in London, which alter over the course of the year. Careful consideration of who, how and when people will use a site therefore helps to maintain aesthetic and amenity value over a period of time. This can occur in newly developed or retrofitted spaces in urban areas and requires a contextual understanding of what was there before, and what can be delivered. Where this can be achieved it helps create valuable and well patronised spaces but when done poorly we see spaces that appear to be uncared for or underused.

——

Reusing industrial land and wasteland for green infrastructure development

One of the most common approaches to green infrastructure development is to rehabilitate former industrial landscapes. Across the UK, Europe and North America land left vacant, derelict or contaminated after industrial change has offered significant opportunities for green infrastructure planners to rethink how interventions in landscape enhancement can promote a revaluation of urban areas. This has included a reflection on how the interactive nature of and communal ties with former industrial sites have changed following their closure. For example, in the former coal mining, shipbuilding and manufacturing sites of northern England and central Scotland there were distinctive communal bonds with the landscape that shaped communities. A number of these ties were severed when the shipyards of Belfast and Glasgow and the coalmines of South Yorkshire closed. From its infancy green infrastructure was proposed as a mechanism to promote landscape rehabilitation in these areas, as it was considered to be economically viable, especially in locations where the landscape held only negative values.

The rethinking of landscape value was a core principle of England's Community Forest network approach to green infrastructure from the early 1990s onwards. Working in the denuded landscapes of the north-east and the north-west of England they engaged communities, local government and businesses to foster buy-in for landscape improvement works. Their work led to significant investment in post-industrial sites to rehabilitate the landscape and make them socially meaningful and functional. The development of Herrington Country Park in Sunderland and West Park in Darlington by the North-East Community Forests demonstrates the value that investing in green infrastructure has added to local communities in areas of deprivation, health inequality and unemployment. The Mersey Forest has engaged in similar activities working with local authorities, communities, schools and the NHS to promote engagement with the landscape through Forest Schools, community tree planting and landscape enhancement work. All of this resulted in a significant shift in how the landscape is viewed locally by communities and by local government in terms of providing additional funding for green infrastructure.

We can also identify a comparable approach to rethinking the links between people and post-industrial landscapes in Belfast. The development of the 10-mile Connswater Greenway has worked with local communities in East Belfast to invest in urban greening, flood mitigation, play provision and educational outreach work to re-establish local communities' value for the landscapes around them. Following the closures of shipbuilding in the Belfast docks many residents of East Belfast lost their attachment to the landscape. However, through ongoing outreach and engagement work the EastSide Partnership and the Connswater Greenway have been able to generate a buy-in from local communities for landscape rehabilitation works.

Internationally we can identify projects in the USA, East Asia and South America that are using a comparable ethos to redevelop derelict land in urban areas. The Atlanta BeltLine project is a 23-mile circular greenway project that makes use of former railyard and railroad infrastructure to create a city-scale greenway (see image on p.114). Working with the City of Atlanta, businesses and representatives of the 45 wards and neighbourhoods in the city, the Atlanta BeltLine development team have brought together engineers, planners, ecologists, real-estate specialists and local communities to rethink how these former industrial locations can be brought back into public use. To date the project has constructed the Eastside Trail, improved storm water management, provided landscape enhancement work in the Historic Fourth Ward Park, improved access and signage to the BeltLine, and promoted biodiversity investment in planting and arboreal management. Each of these interventions has been planned to provide the BeltLine with a range of ecological, social and economic improvements that can benefit individuals, local communities and the city. Although the investment is ongoing, the Atlanta BeltLine can therefore be considered to be the most recent and high-profile project that uses innovation in terms of its form, function and funding to address a variety of social, economic and ecological needs.

The city of Goiania in central Brazil is also engaged in a process of landscape rehabilitation that is focussed on improving the functionality and ecological health of the city's river network. According to the Macambira Anicuns Urban Program all 83 of the city's watercourses suffer from some form of pollution. The most prominent project being undertaken by the city to address this issue is the Macambira Anicuns (LiPMA), a 16.5-mile linear park (covering an area of 25.5 hectares) that includes the provision of two new urban ecological parks that will improve the drainage and restoration of the watercourse, regularise water flow and limit seasonal flooding. It is investing in flora and fauna that minimises the opportunities for mosquito habitats to form (limiting the spread of the Zika virus) and it will also provide much-needed public space for cycling, walking and social

← ↑
New park
development,
Goiania, Brazil.

interaction. The value of the Macambira Anicuns is that it
utilises the underused river corridor and aims to create a location
that is free to access by all members of the community. However,
there are concerns that the project will lead to gentrification
and disenfranchise some members of society. In addition,
commentators have seen the formalisation of a river channel
management plan as limiting the ecological evolution of the
watercourse, which may actually lead to environmental damage
in the future.

Whilst Goiania has looked to green infrastructure as a way of revitalising an undervalued urban river corridor, the city of Detroit has taken a city-wide approach to urban greening in the wake of depopulation and dereliction seen within its boundaries. Working through a community-led approach, large tracts of Detroit have been reimagined as green infrastructure. In many places this has taken the form of urban farms and allotments run by food producing cooperatives and NGOs, whilst other locations have started to actively engage in the planting of flora linked to more effective storm water management through street-scale SuDS. The positive impacts of such projects include real-estate uplift, more effective storm water management and a growing use of the landscape for productive activities, which have led the City of Detroit to allocate funding (US$5 million in total) to help implement further green infrastructure projects. The outcomes of greening work in Detroit are still being evaluated, but as both the city and local communities are rehabilitating formerly derelict spaces, this is viewed as a positive step forward for the long-term use of green infrastructure thinking in the city.

Case Study

The re-naturing of Seoul

The South Korean capital, Seoul, is home to approximately 9.8 million people and is considered one of the most densely populated cities in the world. This has been reflected in its historic development of housing, commercial and transport infrastructure, which interlock across the city fragmenting its green and blue infrastructure. However, as the city has become increasingly congested and polluted its administration started to reconsider the value of Seoul's green infrastructure as a valuable asset promoting a more liveable environment. Two key examples of this process are the conversion of an elevated highway into the Cheonggyecheon River rehabilitation project and the Seoullo 7017 urban skygarden development. The first created a 'green heart' within the centre of Seoul utilising a day lighting process on the Cheonggyecheon River to form a 7-mile urban greenway. Commencing in 2003 the restoration project aimed to provide flood relief, mitigate pollution and develop an inclusive open space that would bring people into an urban oasis in the centre of the city. With an average of over 60,000 users per day the site is a key green infrastructure feature in central Seoul. However, its critics have argued that its cost,

← Sensory Garden at Queen Elizabeth Olympic Park, London, UK.

←↑ Eastside parkways, Atlanta BeltLine, Atlanta, USA.

approximately US$281 million, and a lack of ecological diversity undermines its value to the city. The more recent Seoullo 7017 project has approached the reuse of transport infrastructure in a similar way. It has taken a 983-metre stretch of disused bypass and reformed it as a linear public green space. The project is biodiverse – it holds approximately 24,000 plants – and is intended to make Seoul a greener and less polluted city. In addition to these two projects the city has also increased the amount of public green space in central Seoul by 13,000 square metres, and the 'Greener 1 Million Pyeong programme' has helped initiate a greener school parks programme in 2006, making 376 schools greener by 364,422 square metres and 16 university campuses by 40,360 square metres. Seoul also invested in the Seoul Forest project, which is being developed in Ttukseom district. This is a 0.45-square-mile public-private partnership encouraging residents to plant 420,000 trees and helping to restore the ecological value of the Han River, Jungnang Stream and Cheonggyecheon Stream.

Retrofitting 'landmark' green infrastructure in urban areas

The reuse of urban infrastructure is not the only way in which green infrastructure can be integrated into urban environments. In many cities the retrofitting of existing buildings and infrastructure has been used to increase the proportion of green space and the ecological functionality of urban areas. This can include using more sustainable approaches to heating and cooling buildings such as green roofs, the use of temporary green walls to screen construction activities or more permanent changes to a site that integrate more effective forms of water and biodiversity management. Each of these approaches has its benefits but can also be challenging to deliver. Therefore, effective delivery relies on an awareness of the benefits and the limitations of each approach and an understanding of whether they are appropriate in all locations. In addition, following the lead of the High Line in New York many cities are now looking at how they integrate landmark green infrastructure projects into their urban fabric to increase their proportion of green space, respond to climate change and promote a greener urban branding.

Within London a number of major development companies have started to explore the benefits of greening their construction sites. Through the use of green walls in place of wooden hoardings companies are looking to minimise the visual impact of development and to control the level of pollutants, particularly dust, released from construction sites and the increased traffic associated with deliveries to the site. In addition, they are illustrating their environmental credentials in a crowded market place, which could set their developments apart from other companies in the industry. This approach has been adopted in the external alleyway, the Passage Delanos, which abuts the headquarters of the SNCF railway company in central Paris, which is home to 1400 square metres of green wall providing a visual amenity for the area, as well as water management and cooling benefits due to its size. We can also see a growing investment in green or 'living' walls across university campuses: in Liverpool, Manchester and Belfast in the UK; in Washington DC and Austin in the USA; and in Kunshan and Suzhou in China. Some of these projects are linked to environmental or building designations, for example Leadership in Energy and Environmental Design (LEED); some are reflective of the environmental ethos of an institution; whilst others are attempts to green large institutional buildings to meet sustainability objectives.

There is also a growing number of urban greening projects being proposed by transport organisations and the business community in cities such as London, who are starting to place an economic value on the role that green infrastructure can play. The BIDs in London are leading examples of this process, whereby BID coordinators have worked extensively with local businesses and landowners to levy fees that have been used to invest in green roofs, walls and other forms of urban greening. The Victoria BID has been particularly successful in generating buy-in to support investment in the creation of 25 hectares of green roofs across the area. The Team London Bridge BID has worked with Network Rail, TfL, the NHS and other key landowners to integrate on-street and on-building SuDS to limit the impacts of surface water flooding. The Better Bankside BID is engaged with local companies to integrate street-scale green infrastructure that integrates water management, pollution control and urban biodiversity within street scene improvements. Each of these organisations is, therefore, promoting green infrastructure as a way of managing the local environment to create a more viable location for investment.

Key infrastructure providers including TfL and Network Rail are also starting to engage with the evidence supporting the implementation of green infrastructure. TfL is reviewing the environmental sustainability credentials of its infrastructure and taking steps to integrate green roofs, walls and SuDS systems into the portfolio of buildings. It has also engaged with a 'stations in bloom' programme that works with local communities and station managers to increase the level of biodiversity and plant life on their station platforms and grounds. Network Rail has been more reserved in its use of green infrastructure as it remains concerned about the engineering implications of investment in street trees or SuDS when located near to transport infrastructure. However, it is working with landscape architects, BIDs and the Greater London Authority (GLA) to rethink how to design the public realm around stations to increase their aesthetic and amenity value. This has included working with Team London Bridge to develop the 'Low Line', a series of street improvements that integrate green infrastructure and promote a reuse of underused streets and railway arches for retail and commercial purposes.

A further example of how green infrastructure can be used to create landmark projects is the Thamesmead area of south-west London, where the Peabody Trust, a social housing provider, is working with local communities, environmental experts and utility providers to assess how best to integrate green spaces into their estate. Working at a district scale the Peabody Trust is investing extensively in urban parks, street trees, access and connectivity, and SuDS. Although the area has over 150 hectares of green space and 33,000 trees, Thamesmead is known for its physical isolation due to a lack of transport links, and green infrastructure including the area's waterways is being used to improve the movement of people and wildlife within and across the site. Moreover, the area is using its 4 miles of canals and 3 miles of river frontage to enhance its amenity value. Although the area is considered to have a series of ongoing socio-economic problems, the Peabody Trust's vision is one based around a green network of accessible, socio-culturally valuable and climatically responsive spaces that are functional for all of the area's residents.

One of the most significant investments in green infrastructure has been the development of the Landschaftspark Duisburg Nord in the Ruhr region of Germany. Attracting over 500,000 visitors a year, the site is located on one of the numerous former ironworks in the area and was developed from 1991 onwards. Rather than discarding its industrial heritage, its designers Latz + Partner used this infrastructure as the basis of the park. The site is approximately 180 hectares in size and was partitioned into sectors by Latz + Partners, who were able to create a mosaic landscape of spaces that integrated the industrial nature of the site to create more interactive elements. They also planted around these buildings to produce areas that appeared wild and planted other areas which can be considered managed. The ability of users to transition between the landscapes of the park was a key design feature that allows people to think about the history of the site, its former use as a place of industrial production and its current value as a public park. It is also home to over 700 plant species that provide a constantly diversifying landscape experience, as seen in the 'wild chambers' located in industrial former storage bunkers where nature is left unmanaged compared to the rest of the site.

The retrofitting of green infrastructure around industrial buildings to create a visitor experience that is constantly evolving illustrates the positive ways that greening can be used to rehabilitate derelict spaces. However, such projects can still be considered to be the exception rather than the norm, and in a significant number of European countries green infrastructure is most frequently associated with the development of city-scale parks dating from the seventeenth and eighteenth centuries. In Paris and London, we can identify a series of parks that have become synonymous with the spatial footprint of these cities. Other cities are also known for their city parks: Liverpool's parks have been seen as an essential part of the branding and liveability of the area; Sefton, Calderstones, Newsham and Stanley parks were all developed to improve health and well-being and to provide recreational activities away from the unsanitary parts of the city. More recently the sites have been embedded within development plans, highlighting the value of Liverpool's green infrastructure as a way of attracting investment. This has been done through a 'selling' of the parks as a major public asset that can promote an improved quality of life, as well as helping to manage the city's climate. Although the city council, developers and local communities may hold varying understandings of the value of these spaces there remains an overarching view that Liverpool's parks are a key resource that the city needs to make the best use of.

Thus, where green infrastructure moves from being a site to a landmark within a city or region's landscape, for example the Landschaftspark Duisburg Nord, we can identify a corresponding rise in the value placed on the location and the frequency of use. This can be used to generate additional funding and buy-in for further investment, which helps to maintain aesthetic and amenity value in the long-term.

Case Study

Paris – a green and innovative urban city

Paris has a history of investment in green infrastructure that can be traced back to Haussmann's redesign of the city and which has continued with more recent developments of city and neighbourhood parks. Several high-profile sites have seen green infrastructure retrofitted to improve their social, ecological and economic standing, providing a renewed value to spaces that were previously considered to have little socio-cultural meaning. These sites include the Jardins d'Eole, the Promenade Plantée and the Parc André Citroën. They have all integrated green space into sites that previously had minimal levels of green infrastructure. The Promenade Plantée (also known as the Coulée Verte René-Dumont) is a 3-mile linear park that utilises disused railway infrastructure and has retrofitted the Viaduc des Arts into a multi-purpose green space. It also rethinks the railyard turning circle into a play and recreational area and has increased the proportion of accessible green space in the area. The linear design concept of the

Promenade Plantée was the precursor to the High Line in New York, illustrating the role that the retrofitting of former industrial spaces can have. The Jardins d'Eole provides a comparable example, as the site has been redeveloped from railway infrastructure. Opened in May 2007, the 42,000-square-metre site was redesigned to provide the local community with an accessible, safe and visually diverse green space in what is generally a low-income area. The design of the site retains a small amount of the railway infrastructure; the remainder of the site has been redeveloped to include a variety of garden types increasing the functionality and flexibility of use. Furthermore, there are opportunities for local communities to engage with the site through shared gardening facilities. One of the most significant improvements associated with the project has been the lowering of anti-social behaviour on site as the redeveloped gardens are open on three sides and can thus be observed from homes. Whilst some anti-social behaviour still exists on site this is much lower than during its periods of dereliction. The third example, the Parc André Citroën, is larger in scale at 14 hectares, reflecting the site's former use as a car factory. When it was opened in 1992 it was the largest park to be developed in Paris for over a century. The site is designed to allow the user to move through six themed gardens (blue, green, orange, red, silver and golden) in the north of the site, which house a range of flora and fauna, whilst the park's central area is a large grassed lawn. At the south end of the site a set of greenhouses, shaded gardens, play facilities and water features provide an alternative set of amenities for people to interact with. The redesign of the site has foregrounded the ways in which different user groups utilise urban spaces and has provided a variety of locations where people can interact collectively or individually. Such diversity is viewed as a way of integrating different urban greening approaches into a highly urbanised area to create a mosaic of spaces that provide hard, soft and interactive landscape features.

Case Study

London — Queen Elizabeth Olympic Park

The Queen Elizabeth Olympic Park is a 250-hectare green infrastructure project that integrates urban greening, climate change and urban regeneration principles into a single city-scale site. Built for the London 2012 Olympic Games, the site required environmental rehabilitation due to a history of soil and water contamination linked to former light industrial uses. The site has made explicit use of ecology in the form of wetland and floodplain restoration on the River Lea to mitigate some of the channelisation and flooding impacts of previous development. This has created an evolving seasonal landscape that promotes ecological and hydrological diversity. In addition the site's landscape architects invested extensively in a variety of plant and tree species to ensure that the park is responsive to the variations in London's climate and provides a diverse habitat for bird, mammal and insect species. This diversity has been maintained in the northern sections of the park through an extensive, yet responsive, management regime. The wider green infrastructure network links the Olympic Park to the recently open Walthamstow Wetlands in East London and the London Green Grid, which aims to ensure that people can access the site from a number of locations. It is clear that the high-profile nature of the project and its £9 billion development cost have allowed its architects and landscapers to integrate a more diverse portfolio of spaces and functions into the park, benefitting a great number of people from London and further afield.

Case Study

Bordeaux – waterfront redevelopment

The development of the Garonne river waterfront in Bordeaux-Brazza is a further example of how investments in green infrastructure can deliver city-scale benefits. The 67-hectare waterfront site is located between the river, former railway infrastructure and many of Bordeaux's most historic buildings. The project aimed to revitalise the area's socio-economic value by investing in a high-quality public realm making use of green infrastructure as a key design component. The redeveloped site provides connective routes along the river via a new riverfront park that includes grassed areas and play facilities, and links these with public spaces, such as the 12-hectare Esplanade des Quinconces. It incorporates a road bridge over the river that encourages walking and cycling and creates additional shared space. It also has a series of feature investments including Le Miroir d'eau (the Water Mirror) at the Place de la Bourse, which uses water fountains and artificial mist to create a diverse physical and experiential environment for users.

Case Study

Milan – urban woodlands

The ways in which the city of Milan has engaged with urban forestry and woodlands illustrate how even in higher-density and industrialised cities green infrastructure can be a valuable asset to urban liveability. This is being achieved through

↑ →
Bordeaux
waterfront,
France.

investment in urban forestry via the Parco Sud (181 square
miles) and the Parco Nord (2.5 square miles). Both sites
have invested in urban greening that utilises the planting of
woodland, which transcends the existing boundaries of the city.
To achieve the aim of greening the city a range of authorities at
a local and regional scale has been involved in the formation
and management of the Parco Sud, thus ensuring that its
ecological and agricultural value is maintained. The scale of the
project has also enabled a broader range of funders to become
involved who are buying into the economic value of a greener
and more sustainable Milan. In the Parco Nord, new woodlands
are being created that elongate the green infrastructure
outwards linking the site with a wider network of footpaths,
cycleways and regional resources. Therefore, the site offers
opportunities for users to engage in urban farming, formalised
sports and more informal recreation, which are being integrated
into the site's management plan. Both the Parco Nord and
Parco Sud provide Milan with city-scale green infrastructure
that makes use of the existing landscape resource base and
offers potential for further investment. Their inclusion

↑→
Parco Nord,
Milan, Italy.

and status within the 'Metropolitan Milano' project also
illustrate the city's ambition for further investment in
green infrastructure.

City-scale investment — addressing the 'big' issues

Although we are witnessing the development of a growing
number of landmark green infrastructure projects, we should
not forget that the concept is grounded in understandings of
the diversity of urban form and connectivity. The Emerald
Necklace in Boston is one example of a project that can be
considered to be both. However, when we assess the needs
of a site there is a corresponding requirement to place these
individual spaces in a wider spatial context. This is why cities
such as Stockholm and London have been viewed as being
successful in their provision of green infrastructure, as they
have aligned its development and management with more
strategic environmental and investment issues. Green

infrastructure should therefore be thought of as a key tool in the delivery of a more sustainable landscape and urban development. This includes embedding green infrastructure into the development of other major infrastructure, namely water, utilities, transport, housing and commercial/industrial. Cities, such as London through the developing London Plan, are attempting to deliver such a situation, and are using research undertaken in places such as Malmö in Sweden to frame their inclusion of green infrastructure as a core investment opportunity.

Establishing green infrastructure as an important investment opportunity enables politicians, policy-makers and developers to think more holistically about how green infrastructure can be integrated into urban planning debates. By working at a city or larger scale, green infrastructure can be placed within a wider ecological context. This helps to identify where gaps exist in the current landscape mosaic and provides options for investment in connective features such as cycleways and greenways. It can also illustrate where larger sites such as new parks, riverfront areas and ecologically sensitive infrastructure could make a positive contribution to the provision of amenities, increase economic opportunities and support habitat management. Working at the city scale also enables advocates to promote green infrastructure enhancements that link to long-term investment opportunities. Examples include the provision of new green infrastructure at Trumpington Meadows, near Cambridge, where environmental enhancements were proposed as part of the planning consent for development. Likewise, research from Chicago, Ahmedabad and New York has shown that working at a landscape scale can be a more effective way to manage water resources. This supports the view that a systems or ecosystem services approach that recognises the spatial diversity of supporting, provisioning and regulating services can provide a more knowledgeable grounding for development.

A second positive aspect of thinking at a city or landscape scale is the ability to work more holistically with other disciplines and advocates. This is especially true when green infrastructure strategies or master plans for new developments are being created. The ability to engage planners, architects, engineers and environment and social amenity/service specialists can aid investment in more appropriate forms of green and open space. In many cases, such as the development of the Cambridgeshire Green Infrastructure Strategy, the ability to draw on such a broad range of expertise provided the document with a more robust evidence base that enabled its policy and implementation recommendations to be acceptable to a wider range of stakeholders. The development and execution of the PlaNYC in New York and the strategic investment in Sabarmati Riverfront in Ahmedabad are two further examples where the integration of engineered techniques with green infrastructure approaches have led to significant modifications in the ways in which the physical landscape is managed.

To link these two issues, we must, however, draw on the thematic approaches used to support green infrastructure investment. This can include: addressing storm water and flooding in urban areas, for example in Chicago and Philadelphia; looking to improve access to nature to support healthier lifestyles around Glasgow in Scotland; promoting economic uplift in real-estate investments that utilise green infrastructure in Hong Kong; or the creation of a more liveable environment as many developers and social housing associations are doing in London. A significant number of cities are also looking to invest in green infrastructure to address the heat, pollution and water management issues associated with climate change. These cities include Lahore, Manchester and Los Angeles, whose authorities are all assessing different methods to address the impacts of climate change: how they use new parks and street trees, whether to re-naturalise river channels or invest in green roofs. Lahore in particular has used its historical green wedges to ensure that clean air can circulate within the urban core in a similar way to Stuttgart's 'wind corridors'. Using a thematic angle to engage stakeholders provides opportunities to bring together a greater number of advocates who have expert knowledge of the ecological, social and economic values of green infrastructure at a site and city scale.

Moreover, greenways have been, and continue to be, an important form of green infrastructure that works at an urban scale. They provide access to green spaces across urban areas and can link residential areas with commercial or recreational amenities. This is important in developing an added value to green infrastructure that encourages people to change their behaviour and use these spaces. The development of the Atlanta BeltLine highlights how this can be done, as the project links the downtown area and several of the city's key academic and business institutions with residential neighbourhood and public transport infrastructure. We can see comparable benefits being delivered by the Manhattan Waterfront Greenway in New York and the Silver Jubilee Greenway in London. Greenways also offer planners a way of utilising marginal spaces that are less suitable for development, which can be transformed into areas that promote social interaction and improved health and well-being. Greenways are normally free to access, which is an essential component of promoting social equity in green infrastructure provision. Due to their linear or circular features, they can support climate change mitigation by lowering temperatures due to an increased level of 'green space' being developed, as well as supporting biodiversity and water management in many locations. However, it is important to recognise that greenways should be planned appropriately to meet the needs of the local area. Well-designed greenways can have a transformative impact on the physical and social environment of a city.

Case Study

Circular and linear greening in Shanghai

As Shanghai grows it continues to convert derelict spaces, agricultural land and green spaces to allow new apartments and the infrastructure associated with economic development to be built. One consequence has been a conversion of green infrastructure, which provides important ecological and water management functions, into 'grey' infrastructure. However, the city's strategic plan has made allowances for the provision of green space in the form of new park development, spaces located underneath urban motorways and most significantly through the planning of a series of circular greenways or belts around the city. This includes proposals for 5000 additional hectares of green space to be created. This will increase the overall scale of the city's green infrastructure resource base to over 35 per cent. To achieve this the 'Systematic Planning of Shanghai's Greening' programme uses green wedges/pegs, corridors, rings/loops, parks and forests. The spatial composition of these green infrastructure resources supports the expansion of the city's green network, as well as the management of existing landscape elements such as the Huangpu River, the Suzhou Creek and the city's district-scale parks. Shanghai has also invested extensively in new landmark sites such as the riverfront promenade in Pudong and the Bund on the Shanghai side of the Huangpu. These developments include green walls, parks and play facilities, and wetland vegetation, all of which have been designed to integrate an aesthetic, social and ecological function into these projects. Both projects have been successful in creating spaces that people want to use and which provide essential climatic and flood mitigation benefits.

↑→
Urban greening along transport routes, Shanghai, China.

New Delhi and the National Capital Territory – adapting green infrastructure at a city-regional scale

The Delhi Development Plan identifies a series of landscape-scale green infrastructure resources which are key elements in the city's fight to address climate change, air pollution, flooding mitigation and green space provision. The New Delhi Green Belt ('the ridge') and the Yamuna River are perhaps the most significant resources identified within the document. However, both are subject to ongoing pressures for conversion to meet housing and other infrastructure needs. Moreover, there is evidence that the city's green belt is being encroached upon and converted to housing illegally at such a scale that the city's authorities are unable to manage the process. The conversion of the Yamuna floodplain to provide the accommodation for the 2010 Commonwealth Games and the construction of the Swaminarayan Akshardham Temple on the eastern bank of the river have both led to significant changes in the river's ecology and flood channel. The impact of this has been increased flooding and a greater incidence of pollution as the city's sewage and water supply systems struggle to cope with the added requirements of both developments. In contrast, potentially a more positive form of green infrastructure investment can be seen in the Lutyens-designed Secretariat and India Gate district of the city. These areas saw the development of new government buildings, a change in road layout to a more European boulevard system rather than an organic development of streets, as seen in Old Delhi, and the retention of approximately one-third of the land as green and open space. These spaces – including the gardens on Rajpath, the August Kranti Maidan and the Children's Park at India Gate – have created a connective, multi-functional and landmark parkland due to the range of available recreational activities that are free to the public (unlike other sites in the city). Such spaces are becoming increasingly rare in New Delhi as land is being converted into apartments and private gated communities. The new satellite towns of Gurgaon, Faridabad and Ghaziabad, which are rapidly becoming part of New Delhi rather than part of the NCT, are examples of the privatisation of green infrastructure. As part of the marketing of these new apartments private green spaces are offered as a luxury benefit of ownership. This has in many cases commercialised green infrastructure making it a commodity only available to wealthier residents. As a consequence, the amenity value of the Central Ridge Reserve Park, Lodi

Gardens or Shantivan (Forest of Peace), which is free to use, is becoming increasingly important in its scarcity.

Case Study

Green belts in the UK

Green belts in the UK are noted as being a sacrosanct policy within planning legislation. First proposed for London in the 1930s and legislated more broadly across England in the 1947 Town and Country Planning Act, green belts are a very simple yet complex form of green infrastructure. They are predominantly circular in nature and surround several major urban areas but vary in size, composition, and socio-economic and ecological value. Moreover, in many locations they can be considered to offer access to high-quality landscapes that hold aesthetic, amenity and ecological values. This is not universal across England and as such there are questions being raised over whether they should be retained. Advocates argue that green belts offer a crucial level of protection to green infrastructure at a landscape scale, which may be lost to housing development if legislation is relaxed. These include the Campaign to Protect Rural England (CPRE) which argues that all conversion of green infrastructure is damaging. Alternatively, several think tanks and developers view green belts as a form of elitist protectionism, whereby only the wealthy can afford to live in and enjoy these locations. The Adam Smith Institute has been a staunch supporter of this school of thought, arguing that other development needs, such as housing, are more important than the protection of green spaces of minimal recreational, ecological or productive value. Herein lies one of the key dilemmas pertaining to green belts: due to such variability there is an ongoing conflict over what ecological or social value they hold compared to the wider needs of society for investment in other forms of built infrastructure. An acceptable resolution to this dilemma has not been found, which means that to date green belts remain a protected form of green infrastructure in the UK.

Summary

To ensure that we develop green infrastructure that is accessible, functional and located in the right place we need to reflect on the development context: the physical environment, social needs, economic imperatives and ecological structure of a location. Through such assessment we can determine what resources are currently available and what forms of green infrastructure could be developed. This leads to a series of interesting and interlocking questions, which reflect on how we reuse, retrofit or create new green and blue spaces, whether they should meet specific localised needs or be used to develop landmark projects, and whether we are working at a local, neighbourhood or city scale. Each of these issues helps to guide the development of green infrastructure, providing options for developers, decision-makers and planners evaluating the best form of landscape enhancement. The chapter has described a range of examples where bolder investments have been implemented and are considered successes. It has also illustrated some of the constraints in terms of finding a balance between the location and focus of a green infrastructure investment and meeting the needs of its desired user groups. Green infrastructure planning should therefore be thought of as an evolutionary process that makes best use of existing resources to bring together a range of advocates to deliver more sustainable forms of urban development.

Chapter 6

How Do We Plan for Green Infrastructure? Linking Policy, Guidance and Practice

The previous chapters discussed what green infrastructure is, what it looks like and how it can be developed in different geographical and socio-economic contexts. To support this debate, this chapter outlines how we take the principles of green infrastructure and think about them within a policy/practice arena. It explores examples of green infrastructure policy and how it has changed over time, and identifies where gaps remain in the discussion about green infrastructure by politicians, developers and decision-makers. By reflecting on these questions, we can identify good practice and where change is needed to promote investment in green infrastructure.

Policy formation is a complex process that aims to generate a level of consensus between stakeholders to support the delivery of strategic objectives. In most locations competing social, ecological and economic agendas are visible, which can lead to conflicts regarding the focus and implementation of green infrastructure. Where land values or economic development are paramount to policy formation, for example in India and China, it can be difficult to engage politicians and developers in conversations about the added value that green infrastructure can deliver. In such locations, it has fallen to advocates to raise the visibility of green infrastructure through evidence-sharing, engagement and the development of guidance that can subsequently be used by government to shape decision-making. How such advocacy influences policy formation is, however, varied; in cities around the world, politicians, developers and planners engage in different ways with the growing evidence supporting investment in green infrastructure.

Several key issues can be identified as promoting the use of green infrastructure in policy. These include an understanding of how green infrastructure can be implemented at a number of scales (see Chapter 2) and the range of socio-economic and ecological benefits it can deliver (see Chapters 3–5). It can also be considered to engage stakeholders from public, private and environment sector organisations providing policy-makers with a more robust baseline to help create their visions for a location. However, managing this process can be difficult if the competing agendas of different stakeholders cannot be moderated. The following sections debate these issues illustrating where good practice in green infrastructure policy-making can be identified.

Global planning policy supporting green infrastructure

	Main policy instrument	Main delivery arena	Focus of green infrastructure development
UK	National Planning Policy Framework (NPPF)	Sub-regional, local planning authority and local environmental agency-led	Biodiversity, social cohesion/community engagement, water management, climate change, economic development, health and well-being
Germany	Regional Plans	Regional/Länder, city government-led	Sustainable transport, ecological conservation/biodiversity, recreation, flood/water management, recreation, health and well-being
USA	Regional and city-scale policies/strategies, e.g. PlaNYC, EPA guidance (none statutory)	City-scale development strategies, county and community-scale projects/strategies, EPA guidance	Storm water/flood management, landscape-scale conservation, biodiversity, recreation, health and well-being, real estate/economic value

China	City-scale master plans, plans for new developments and urban extensions	New city master plans, private developer master plans, consultant-led plans, strategic guidance from city government	Transport, economic development, water management, social well-being, aesthetics, sponge/eco-city, pollution control
India	National Urban Greening Guidelines (2014)	State- and city-scale strategic development plans, private developer master plans	Water provision/ management, economic development, real-estate values, aesthetics, conservation, recreation, biodiversity

At what scale should we plan for green infrastructure?

Planning effectively for green infrastructure requires an understanding of how environmental functions and humans interact with the landscape at a number of scales. This includes reflecting on how individuals use a specific location, as well as discussing how water systems or habitats work at a city or regional scale. Within green infrastructure it is important to ensure that these discussions are aligned to create a suite of policies, guidance notes or implementation programmes that link investment to different forms of urban need. This is crucial to the effectiveness of policy, as it allows policy-makers and other green infrastructure advocates to promote the local, neighbourhood and city-scale benefits of specific interventions, and enables them to plan accordingly. Working within such a system should enable planners to work more holistically with stakeholders to ensure that investments are meeting the aspirations of communities and businesses without compromising the functionality of the environment resource base.

Unfortunately, it is not always easy to align the agendas of stakeholders whose mandates are focussed on different outcomes. Consequently, we are seeing a growing number of green infrastructure strategies being developed at the city and regional scale. Whilst this provides green infrastructure advocates with a range of options through which to invest in landscape enhancement projects, conflicts arise when these policies, strategies or guidance notes are deemed to be unaligned. Where strategies and policies are developed at the local scale they can be focussed on a discrete site or neighbourhood, which provides a more detailed analysis of the local context and the potential value of green infrastructure in these locations. Locally focussed plans may not consider the broader value or implications of investing in green infrastructure such as ongoing maintenance costs, alignment with other resources or the impacts of investment on city-scale environmental systems. In the UK this can be seen in the developing Neighbourhood Plans in Kennington, Oval and Vauxhall in South London and in Wilmslow in Cheshire. Within both plans green infrastructure is seen as offering health, well-being, economic and ecological benefits to local communities, but there is a potential lack of strategic thinking about how they provide broader benefits or fit with city-scale interventions.

Due to the increasingly discrete focus of local green infrastructure plans it is more common to see city-scale strategies being developed that take in a broader spatial area. Such guidance has been developed in New York, Philadelphia, Copenhagen and London and considers the ways in which the principles of green infrastructure, connectivity, access to nature, the delivery of multiple benefits and a more sustainable approach to landscape management can be embedded within a more strategic investment plan. However, to achieve consensus at such a scale requires a longer time period, as a greater number of issues including stakeholder engagement, land ownership, funding, and competing built environment objectives need to be moderated. It is therefore crucial in the creation of city-scale green infrastructure plans to have effective leadership that can shape these competing agendas. The development of PlaNYC is one example of such leadership where the former Mayor of New York, Michael Bloomberg, helped generate buy-in for the plan. We can identify a similar process with the creation of the Atlanta BeltLine, where political and business support from within the city has been critical in creating a supporting policy environment to help deliver the project. Unfortunately, due to land prices and the nature of real-estate speculation, it has not always been easy to embed green infrastructure into policy if or when economic development objectives may be compromised. It can be difficult to convince stakeholders that the creation of new parks, waterways and other forms of green infrastructure should be given equal prominence with more conventional built infrastructure. This has historically been the situation in Liverpool where green space has been considered as a secondary investment priority. More recently we have started to see a shift to include green infrastructure in city planning, as the benefits of climate change adaptation, health and flood management have been made clear to the city's leadership.

Arguably green infrastructure planning has been most successful at a city-regional or landscape scale. From its initial development by the Conservation Fund in the USA and the UK's Community Forest Partnerships there has been a greater number of strategies and policies developed which focus on a landscape approach to green infrastructure investment than smaller-scale projects. The discussions of green infrastructure in the Chesapeake Bay area of Maryland or the Mersey Forest's plan for the Liverpool city-region are two examples of plans focussing on this scale. In both, the authors were able to address landscape-scale issues associated with water management, urban forestry, health and well-being, and the integration of green infrastructure into new developments because they were able to identify the benefits, and to show where gaps were visible in the green infrastructure network. Over a prolonged period both organisations have worked with environmental, public and private stakeholders to create strategic plans that have led to significant delivery of green infrastructure. More recently we have seen comparable approaches being taken in Cambridgeshire in the UK with the development of the Second Green Infrastructure Strategy and in the management strategies for the Parco Nord and Parco Sud in Milan. It must, however, be noted that, as with city-scale strategies, gaining consensus for regional investment strategies is often a complex and protracted exercise.

Case Study ### The Atlantic Gateway proposals for Liverpool – Manchester corridor

The Atlantic Gateway project is a multi-partner project that engaged local planning authorities, Local Enterprise Partnerships (LEPs), private businesses and other public bodies to engineer investment into the Liverpool–Manchester city-region covering approximately 700 square miles. Focussed on the River Mersey and the Manchester Ship Canal, the Atlantic Gateway proposes investment in commercial and infrastructure development to encourage economic investment. Aligned with the creation of new built infrastructure a corresponding green infrastructure strategy has been developed: the *Atlantic Gateway Parklands: The Landscape of Prosperity* document proposes a series of localised environmental enhancement projects associated with parks, woodlands and wetlands that are aligned with more strategic interventions in water quality and flood prevention. One of the key aims of the strategy is to develop an accessible, diverse and interactive landscape. Green infrastructure is proposed within the Atlantic Gateway project as a way of supporting environmental sustainability, promoting an increased awareness of the benefits that landscape enhancement can deliver and creating a physically attractive location for investment.

Does green infrastructure policy actually work?

It is sometimes questioned whether having a green infrastructure policy actually makes any material difference to investment in landscape enhancement. We can say with certainty though that through the development of green infrastructure policies, strategies and guidance, the concept is being debated as a key policy area, which has allowed advocates to plan for and deliver more investment in landscape enhancement. This is invariably tied to the local political context with stronger advocacy, such as in Atlanta or Paris, leading to green infrastructure being delivered. The firm positioning of green infrastructure on the planning, design and development agenda has allowed it to maintain a political presence over a 20-year period as the most frequently discussed form of 'landscape planning' in urban development.

We can also review the uptake of green infrastructure ideas from their conceptual development in the early 2000s, into policy and finally into the implementation and management practices that we currently see. In the UK, the benefits of this are apparent in the recently revised National Planning Policy Framework (NPPF), the developing London Plan and the use of innovative SuDS investments. For examples, see *Guidance on the Construction of SuDS* (C768, 2017), produced by the Construction Industry Research and Information Association (CIRIA), and the CIRIA-authored *The SuDS Manual* (C753, 2015). We can also identify comparable green infrastructure principles within the master plan for the Beijing Olympic Park and within the ongoing management practices of the classical gardens of Suzhou. We see green infrastructure being embedded within the participatory budget of the Mairie de Paris and the growing awareness of NBS in Valladolid in Spain and Izmir in Turkey. The development of strategies in northern American cities such as Philadelphia and New York also illustrate a growing awareness of the benefits that green infrastructure can deliver, especially when linked to storm water. In each of these locations the support given to green infrastructure within policy through the evidence presented in strategies has helped shape the implementation of landscape enhancements in the forms of SuDS, street tree investments, new parks, green walls and green roofs. This is a positive shift that has occurred over the past decade and has seen green infrastructure move from something that could be developed into something that is considered as a first principle of investment.

It should be added, however, that despite this shift not all locations that have green infrastructure strategies, policies or guidance have been able to successfully deliver these agendas. In India, for example, the central government mandate of economic development (currently around 9 per cent per annum) has undermined the provision, funding and management of green infrastructure. Likewise, in cities in China and Hong Kong where the availability of land and the subsequent costs of real estate are prohibitive, investment in green infrastructure, as a consequence, does not get delivered. These locations do, however, appear to be in the minority, as where a supportive policy environment exists, such as in Berlin (see Lachmund's *Greening Berlin*, 2013), there is frequently a corresponding process of implementation. Philadelphia is a further example, where significant steps have been taken in embedding green infrastructure into the city's 'Green City, Clean Waters' plan and this mandate has been supported politically. These examples should be examined to help identify good practice for investment.

Case Study   **The Ahmedabad Development Plan**

The Ahmedabad Development Plan was developed by the AUDA and the AMC to shape the economic and environmental vision for this Indian city. The population of Ahmedabad, Gujarat's economic centre, grew to an estimated eight million people in 2018, and is predicted to continue to rise. This has caused tensions with the city's planning, development and environmental sectors as new transport, commercial and housing infrastructure is required to meet the needs of an expanding population. Whilst the Ahmedabad Development Plan accounts for these investments, it also makes clear that there is a need for a corresponding financing of green infrastructure investment to help mitigate the changing climatic conditions associated with growth. Through a series of recommendations, the plan calls for the development of a hierarchy of green infrastructure sites, including the Sabarmati Riverfront redevelopment and public parks. These are supplying a city-scale 'green' resource for its population and are to be supported through additional investments in Ahmedabad's lake system, street trees and 'urban groves', which should be planted on all development sites before construction begins and retained on completion. These investments are seen as providing options for both public and private developers to ensure that green infrastructure is integrated into the city's urban form. Although there have been objections – by businesses, academics and developers – to the types of green infrastructure being implemented, the plan shows a clear intention from AUDA and the AMC to align urban greening with more traditional forms of urban infrastructure to help create a more sustainable city.

Case Study

The London Plan

The consultation supporting the development of the next London Plan highlights the value placed upon green infrastructure by the London Assembly and the Mayor of London. When compared to the now-revoked Regional Spatial Strategy for London, the current iteration has a significantly more detailed and analytical approach to green infrastructure provision. The 2017–18 draft plan embeds green infrastructure in several policies related to multi-functional landscapes, sustainable town centre design, urban greening, and air and water quality/pollution management. It is also supported by a specific green infrastructure chapter within the plan outlining an extensive evidence base highlighting the social, economic and ecological value of investing in landscape enhancement. This covers the role of green infrastructure in supporting real-estate uplift, improving the quality of life and health of residents, and the use of urban greening to address the impacts of transport and construction pollution across the city. Interestingly the latest iteration of the plan explicitly highlights the symbiotic relationship between the physical environment, its functionality and aesthetic quality, the economic prosperity of the city, and the social well-being of the people who live and work in London. This establishes a value for green infrastructure which has been absent from previous London Plans, suggesting that the advocacy and communication of evidence to the London Assembly has been influential in shaping its vision.

Who should be involved in developing and paying for green infrastructure?

There is an assumption, especially in the UK, that central or local government is responsible for developing green infrastructure. Whilst this has historically been true, with local planning authorities using their core grants from central government and local taxes to fund green infrastructure investment, this is no longer a certainty. As a consequence, we are starting to witness a growing diversity in terms of who is planning and who is funding green infrastructure in the UK and globally.

The key stakeholders in this debate remain local government, developers, communities and businesses. However, the relationship between each and the development of green infrastructure has evolved. This reflects the growing awareness of the socio-economic and ecological value of green infrastructure and the returns that can be expected from investment in urban greening. For example, PlaNYC states that although green infrastructure may not deliver the same level of economic return as other forms of grey or built infrastructure, it will potentially see a proportionally higher rate of return (per cent increase versus total cost of investment), thus lowering the overall cost to the city. Consequently, we can identify developers in the UK, China and India who are starting to engage with green infrastructure as a way of improving the quality of their developments be they apartments, commercial premises or public spaces. Due to their economic focus, it is interesting to see developers starting to plan for green walls, SuDS and the greening of public spaces, as a way of increasing the value of their 'product'. Grosvenor Estates in the UK is one such organisation engaged in this process through its *Living Cities: Our Approach to Practice*. Such commercialisation of green infrastructure is also being discussed by local government in the UK as a way of ensuring that parks and open spaces make a financial contribution to city budgets. In places such as Sheffield, Newcastle and Liverpool this has meant allowing businesses to locate themselves in green spaces and for charges to be levied on the use of these premises or parks for events. However, it is not viable to commercialise all green spaces so each local government or landowner will need to take account of what may be possible on a site-by-site basis.

Moreover, we are now seeing a greater level of local government and private capital investment in public spaces helping to fund green infrastructure. This includes the retrofitting of buildings with green walls and roofs but also the creation of public-private partnerships, such as the ones delivering the Atlanta BeltLine in the USA or the Atlantic Gateway in the UK. Where such partnerships are developed there is scope to align the strategic needs of local government and the commercial tendencies of private enterprise. However, the public and campaigning organisations often raise concerns regarding the transparency of such agreements, especially where changes in use or access to green infrastructure occur. The ongoing discussion of street tree management in Sheffield is one example where the costs of maintenance are not necessarily equated to the socio-economic or ecological value attributed to urban green infrastructure by a local authority. Clarity is needed to ensure that developments do not downgrade the benefits of green space to the public in favour of private gains.

While public and private stakeholders are central to the creation and management of green infrastructure, there is scope for the inclusion of community groups and environmental organisations to act as key delivery and management stakeholders in these debates. For example, organisations such as the CNT in Chicago and Trees for Cities in London often have extensive local knowledge and are potentially more reflective of local needs than public or private institutions. Space should therefore be made to enable such groups to engage with the strategy and, where appropriate, the implementation of green infrastructure. The Community Forest Partnership in the UK, specifically the Mersey Forest and Manchester: City of Trees, and the Conservation Fund in the USA are examples of organisations who have been able to work with communities (and local government) to generate buy-in for investment in green infrastructure. Each has used climate change, health and well-being, recreation and play, and environmental management to help focus their engagement with different communities. There is also a corresponding debate addressing whether communities should be afforded the responsibility of managing and funding green infrastructure. This needs careful consideration, as not all groups have the experience, knowledge or time to undertake such roles. Even where community asset transfers are used they can be undermined over time without additional support from more experienced landscape or community development professionals. They do, however, work when transfers are associated with allotments or community gardening projects, as these are seen to sustain a higher level of community engagement. Every effort should be made to generate consensus around what green infrastructure should be developed and where and how it can be paid for when a wide range of stakeholders are involved in investment discussions.

Cambridgeshire's Green Infrastructure Strategy

The Second Cambridgeshire Green Infrastructure Strategy was developed over a two-year period and was led by Cambridge Horizons, a quasi-non-governmental development agency, in conjunction with environmental and local government stakeholders. The second iteration of the strategy built on the first but extended the area of discussion to the whole of Cambridgeshire (Fenland had been omitted from the original strategy). It also drew on a wider range of stakeholder experiences and engagement from across the public and environment sectors. This provided the steering group with expertise in planning, implementation, ecological and socio-economic development, which helped to shape the principles, structure and proposed recommendations of the strategy. It also created a valuable route into local government, as representatives of each of the five local planning authorities (East Cambridgeshire, South Cambridgeshire, Huntingdonshire, Fenland and the City of Cambridge) were engaged from its inception. This allowed the evolving focus of the strategy to be reported to each authority's elected members and officers, who provided an additional forum for discussion, the interrogation of evidence and the inclusion of locally specific investments into the strategy. The second iteration took the initial strategy as a starting point in terms of identifying key development principles and projects and extended these through a county-wide process of analysis and subsequent public consultation. The outcome was a document that focussed on reversing the decline in biodiversity, adapting to and mitigating climate change, promoting sustainable economic development, and supporting health and well-being. These principles were then aligned with a series of neighbourhood, local and county-scale investment opportunities to provide a spatial and thematic approach to investment. Since 2011, many stakeholders have used it as a supplementary planning document to help shape local policy and practice.

Summary

The variability of green infrastructure policy around the world reflects the variation also identified in practice. Where strong leadership and advocacy exists, there is frequently an increased level of investment and management for green infrastructure. However, the development context and the role of communities and private business also need to be considered as they can play key roles in the evidencing and funding of urban greening projects and have vested interests in promoting economic prosperity and sustainable places to live, work and recreate. Where the agendas of such disparate stakeholders can be aligned, as in Paris, London and Philadelphia, we see the creation of appropriate and deliverable green infrastructure. This is, however, an evolving process that requires ongoing engagement to reinforce the principles, options and benefits of green infrastructure for a given location. It should be noted that a growing number of cities have created and are delivering green infrastructure that meets strategic and local needs, and which is financed through a variety of different public, private and community models.

Chapter 7

**What Next for
Green Infrastructure?**

This final chapter summarises some of the key challenges facing green infrastructure planning and proposes a series of ways in which its principles can be embedded within policy and practice at different scales and in a number of locations. These illustrate the benefits of investing in green infrastructure, and how alternative approaches to policy development and subsequent implementation can promote more sustainable places. It also includes a reflection on the ways in which green infrastructure can be funded and concludes by setting out where green infrastructure planning may go next. The chapter will act as a reassurance for those working in green infrastructure and a call to arms for those currently thinking about what value it could add to their development.

The future management of green infrastructure
The previous chapters highlighted how green infrastructure is being managed in order to deliver a range of social, ecological and economic benefits. These discussions illustrate the variability of approaches taken, which is a positive sign for the future development and management of green infrastructure, as all investment needs to be responsive to the local socio-economic and environmental context, a view grounded within the principles of green infrastructure planning. As a consequence, where effective landscape enhancement, urban greening and investment in green and blue spaces has occurred it can be viewed as being appropriate to the local context. How we continue to ensure such an alignment occurs is, however, more

complex. We need to look beyond the traditional in terms of how plans are developed, who manages and who pays for green infrastructure, and think more strategically about who has the expertise and experience to lead the development of new guidance, policies and implementation plans. Invariably this will involve local government but we also need to ensure that the environment sector (the biggest advocates for green infrastructure to date), utilities and construction companies, businesses, the health profession and communities are on board. Through more integrated green infrastructure strategies, implementation and subsequent management, we will potentially see a more sustainable and long-term approach to urban management that respects human-environmental interactions and views the landscape as a valuable resource. There are many ways to achieve this, including more effective partnership working, increased engagement with local knowledge and the development of strong advocacy or leadership from within political and business communities. Where each of these can be generated and maintained there is scope for innovative, high-quality and multi-functional green infrastructure to be developed. We can identify examples from across Europe, North America and Asia where this is happening, and these projects, policies and advocates should be used as exemplars to support other cities aiming to create green infrastructure. We should not forget, however, that evidence, policy and implementation programmes take time and should be seen as a longer-term pathway to more sustainable forms of development.

Future investment in green infrastructure

A range of new approaches to fund green infrastructure have been identified as offering opportunities for various stakeholders to pay for and manage investment in the landscape. The diversity of possible stakeholders from the public, private, voluntary and community sectors raises questions over who are the best people to manage our environmental resources. In the UK and USA this has been exacerbated by the rescinding of funding for landscape protection and management, meaning that government officials and environmental specialists are having to think innovatively about the financial future of green infrastructure. Cities such as Liverpool, Newcastle and even London in the UK have all started to assess how they will fund their green spaces in the coming years. Out of this discussion has come an acceptance, especially within the UK, that central government funding can no longer be relied upon. Thus we have witnessed an increase in the number of discussions focussed on the sale, transfer of ownership or sponsorship of green infrastructure by businesses or the development industry. This has coincided with a growing awareness by construction companies that (a) they can make higher profits by investing in greener and more sustainable forms of development and (b) investment in green infrastructure can, in many cases, be cheaper than engineered solutions. Changes in zoning and taxation could be used to fund green infrastructure if local governments act more strategically to align urban greening principles with wider development debates. We are also seeing green infrastructure start to embed itself in business thinking with companies viewing the added value of a productive workforce or 'sustainable' brands associated with green infrastructure as marketable. In addition, there are numerous examples, including New York's community gardens and 'Million Trees' project, the Parks Trust model associated with Milton Keynes in the UK, the BIDs in London and the Parisian Mayoral Participatory Budget, which illustrate a movement away from established government-led forms of investment and management towards a more environmentally focussed process of funding. Each of these projects has worked because it has been able to identify aspects of green infrastructure planning that are desirable to alternative partners or communities, enabling resources to be moved from one organisation or area of planning to another. Whilst this raises questions over who should manage the landscapes around us it shows that non-traditional and potentially non-expert stakeholders can successfully fulfil these roles. However, there remains a need in such conversations to reflect on the context of a green infrastructure resource to ask whether or not a set of stakeholders can actually manage it. This dilemma has been highlighted with Community Asset

Transfers of green spaces in the UK; once community groups have been provided with the full legal, administrative and management regulations associated with a transfer they may not be willing or able to take control of a park or nature area, possibly lacking the knowledge, skills or time to manage these spaces. There are opportunities to think about how advocates can draw on the needs of business communities through direct payments, sponsorship or Public-Private Partnerships. Significant changes are occurring in how we fund and manage green infrastructure, which are leading to a level of reflection not witnessed previously. Out of this, more innovative and responsive approaches to funding may be generated leading to long-term funding which is more sustainable.

The future praxis of green infrastructure planning
It seems clear to many in the field of green infrastructure planning that its future development of policy and implementation will look very different to the current approaches to development, management and evaluation. Existing funding streams can no longer be relied upon, the value placed on green spaces by the public, by private enterprises and government is diversifying, and our knowledge of the complexity of environmental systems is constantly growing. Therefore, our approach to green infrastructure planning is evolving and could be considered to hold a pluralistic set of values that other forms of development no longer hold. Who gets to decide how green infrastructure develops in the future is part of this debate and raises questions regarding both the capacity and knowledge of various public, private and community stakeholders to manage the landscape effectively.

To successfully achieve a continued advocacy for green infrastructure we can reflect upon the following agenda, which can be used to structure how we deliver investment in sustainable urban landscapes:

- Green infrastructure should be considered as a basic principle of all development in urban areas. If this can be achieved then it will be discussed alongside other forms of infrastructure, and should be planned into our cities from the start.

- Planners, decision-makers and developers need to be aware of the socio-economic and ecological functions and benefits of green infrastructure. Through an engagement with the research and projects focussing on green infrastructure it becomes clear how it can address climate change, health, biodiversity, recreation, transport and economic development needs in different cities across the world.

- Green infrastructure comes in many shapes and sizes and should not be considered as a one-size-fits-all approach to development. Different projects require different solutions so an awareness of the diversity of green infrastructure is critical to its appropriate use.

- Green infrastructure can address discrete or localised issues but can also be developed as part of a wider investment strategy or landmark project. Planners, decision-makers and developers should therefore be aware of the flexibility of approaches that green infrastructure can provide to meet the changing needs of urban areas.

- Engaging with expertise and local knowledge from across environmental, engineering and built environment disciplines will provide a more robust basis for investment in green infrastructure. Likewise architects and designers should be more actively engaged in this process to discuss the look, interactivity and functionality of an investment.

- All advocates need to think innovatively about how to fund investment. Recently we have seen a growing number of funding mechanisms that span public, private and community approaches, which can be used to mitigate falling government spending on environmental enhancement.

Finally, we need to maintain an understanding that green infrastructure is all about the political, social, economic and ecological context. With an understanding of each we can reflect upon how green infrastructure can meet the needs of different locations to provide multi-functional benefits. Therefore, if we as planners, designers, developers and decision-makers engage with the principles of green infrastructure, learn from best practice and utilise each of these recommendations we can develop more interactive, functional and sustainable places.

Abbreviations

ALGG	All London Green Grid
AMC	Ahmedabad Municipal Corporation
ANGSt	Accessible Natural Greenspace Standards
AUDA	Ahmedabad Urban Development Authority
BAME	Black-Asian-Minority Ethnic
BID	Business Improvement District
CCG	Clinical Commissioning Groups
CIAT	Countryside In and Around Towns
CIL	Community Infrastructure Levy
CIRIA	Construction Industry Research and Information Association
CMAP	Chicago Metropolitan Agency for Planning
CNT	Center for Neighborhood Technology
CPRE	Campaign to Protect Rural England
DDA	Delhi Development Authority
DEFRA	Department for Environment, Food and Rural Affairs
DNR	Department of Natural Resources
ELC	European Landscape Convention
ENGO	Environmental Non-Governmental Organisation
EPA	Environmental Planning Agency
ES	Ecosystem Services
GCV	Glasgow and Clyde Valley
GI	Green Infrastructure
GLA	Greater London Authority
GU	Green Urbanism
HGF	Housing Growth Fund
IMCSD	Inter-Ministerial Committee on Sustainable Development
LEED	Leadership in Energy and Environmental Design
LEP	Local Enterprise Partnership
LLDC	London Legacy Development Corporation
LOCOG	London Organising Committee of the Olympic and Paralympic Games
LPA	Local Planning Authority
MIT	Massachusetts Institute of Technology
MWRD	Metropolitan Water Reclamation District
NBS	Nature-Based Solutions
NCT	National Capital Territory
NDD	Nature-deficit disorder
NGO	Non-Governmental Organisation
NHS	National Health Service
NPPF	National Planning Policy Framework
ODPM	Office of the Deputy Prime Minister
OPDC	Olympic Park Development Corporation

Abbreviations

PFI	Public Finance Initiative
PPP	Public-Private Partnership
PPS/PPG	Planning Policy Statement/Planning Policy Guidance
RDA	Regional Development Agency
RSS	Regional Spatial Strategy
RTPI	Royal Town Planning Institute
S106	Section 106 planning consent agreement/payment
SIP	Singapore Industrial Park
SRFDCL	Sabarmati Riverfront Development Corporation Ltd
SuDS	Sustainable Urban Drainage Systems
TCPA	Town and Country Planning Association
TfL	Transport for London
UK NEA	UK Natural Ecosystem Assessment
VALUE	Valuing Attractive Landscapes in the Urban Economy
WFD	Water Framework Directive
XJTLU	Xi'an Jiaotong-Liverpool University

Bibliography

Journal articles

Ahern, J. (1995). 'Greenways as a planning strategy'. *Landscape and Urban Planning*, 33(1–3), 131–55.

Ahern, J. (2013). 'Urban landscape sustainability and resilience: the promise and challenges of integrating ecology with urban planning and design'. *Landscape Ecology*, 28(6), 1203–12.

Andersson, E., Barthel, S., Borgström, S., Colding, J., Elmqvist, T., Folke, C. and Gren, A. (2014). 'Reconnecting cities to the biosphere: stewardship of green infrastructure and urban ecosystem services'. *Ambio*, 43(4), 445–53.

Bentsen, P., Mygind, E. and Randrup, T.B. (2009). 'Towards an understanding of udeskole: education outside the classroom in a Danish context'. *Education*, 3–13, 37(1), 29–44. http://doi.org/10.1080/03004270802291780 (accessed 21 August 2018).

Cho, M.-R. (2010).'The politics of urban nature restoration: the case of Cheonggyecheon restoration in Seoul, Korea'. *International Development Planning Review*, 32(2), 145–65. http://doi.org/10.3828/idpr.2010.05 (accessed 21 August 2018).

Connop, S., Vandergert, P., Eisenberg, B., Collier, M.J., Nash, C., Clough, J. and Newport, D. (2016). 'Renaturing cities using a regionally-focused biodiversity-led multifunctional benefits approach to urban green infrastructure'. *Environmental Science and Policy*, 62, 99–111. http://doi.org/10.1016/j.envsci.2016.01.013 (accessed 21 August 2018).

Fábos, J. G. (2004). Greenway planning in the United States: its origins and recent case studies'. *Landscape and Urban Planning*, 68(2–3), 321–42.

Hansen, R. and Pauleit, S (2014). 'From multifunctionality to multiple ecosystem services? A conceptual framework for multifunctionality in green infrastructure planning for urban areas'. *Ambio*, 43(4), 516–29.

Jerome, G., Mell, I.C. and Shaw, D. (2017). 'Re-defining the characteristics of environmental volunteering: creating a typology of community-scale green infrastructure'. *Environmental Research*, 158, 399–408. http://doi.org/10.1016/j.envres.2017.05.037 (accessed 21 August 2018).

Jim, C. and Chen, W.Y (2006). 'Impacts of urban environmental elements on residential housing prices in Guangzhou (China)'. *Landscape and Urban Planning*, 78(4), 422–34.

Kabisch, N., Frantzeskaki, N., Pauleit, S., Naumann, S., Davis, M., Artmann, M., Haase, D., Knapp, S., Korn, H., Stadler, J., Zaunberger, K., and Bonn, A. (2016). 'Nature-based solutions to climate change mitigation and adaptation in urban areas: perspectives on indicators, knowledge gaps, barriers, and opportunities for action'. *Ecology and Society*, 21(2), 39. http://doi.org/10.5751/ES-08373-210239 (accessed 21 August 2018).

Kirkman, R., Noonan, D.S and Dunn, S.K. (2012). 'Urban transformation and individual responsibility: the Atlanta BeltLine'. *Planning Theory*, 11(4), 418–34.

Kumar, P., Geneletti, D. and Nagendra, H. (2016). 'Spatial assessment of climate change vulnerability at city scale: a study in Bangalore, India'. *Land Use Policy*, 58, 514–32.

Lennon, M., Scott, S., Collier, C. and Foley, K. (2017). 'The emergence of green infrastructure as promoting the centralisation of a landscape perspective in spatial planning—the case of Ireland'. *Landscape Research*, 42(2), 146–63.

Lindsey, G., Maraj, M. and Kuan, S. (2001). 'Access, equity, and urban greenways: an exploratory investigation'. *The Professional Geographer*, 53(3), 332–46.

Meerow, S. and Newell, J.P. (2017). 'Spatial planning for multifunctional green infrastructure: growing resilience in Detroit'. *Landscape and Urban Planning*, 159, 62–75. http://doi.org/10.1016/j.landurbplan.2016.10.005 (accessed 21 August 2018).

Mell, I.C. (2017a). 'Green infrastructure: reflections on past, present and future praxis'. *Landscape Research*, 42(1), 135–45.

Mell, I.C. (2017b). 'Greening Ahmedabad?: creating a resilient Indian city using a green infrastructure approach to investment'. *Landscape Research*, 1–26. http://doi.org/10.1080/01426397.2017.1314452 (accessed 21 August 2018).

Mell, I.C. and Sturzaker, J. (2014). 'Sustainable urban development in tightly constrained areas: a case study of Darjeeling, India'. *International Journal of Urban Sustainable Development*, 6(1). http://doi.org/10.1080/19463138.2014.883994 (accessed 21 August 2018).

Moreira, J. de F.R. and Silva, C.A. da (2012) 'Paisagem Urbana e áreas verdes: contexto dos parques urbanos de Goiânia'. *Boletim Goiano de Geografia*, 32, 2, 239–54.

Nagendra, H. and Gopal, D. (2010). 'Street trees in Bangalore: Density, diversity, composition and distribution'. *Urban Forestry and Urban Greening*, 9(2), 129–37.

Nassauer, J. (1995). 'Culture and changing landscape structure'. *Landscape Ecology*, 10(4), 229–37. http://doi.org/10.1007/BF00129257 (accessed 21 August 2018).

Pauleit, S., Slinn, P., Handley, J. and Lindley, S. (2003). 'Promoting the natural greenstructure of towns and cities: English Nature's accessible "Natural Greenspace Standards" model'. *Built Environment*, 29(2), 157–70.

Pretty, J., Peacock, J., Sellens, M. and Griffin, M. (2005). 'The mental and physical health outcomes of green exercise'. *International Journal of Environmental Health Research*, 15(5), 319–37.

Schmelzkopf, K. (2002). 'Incommensurability, land use, and the right to space: community gardens in New York City'. *Urban Geography*, 23(4), 323–43.

Weber, T., Sloan, A. and Wolf, J. (2006). 'Maryland's Green Infrastructure Assessment: development of a comprehensive approach to land conservation'. *Landscape and Urban Planning*, 77(1–2), 94–110.

Books

Austin, G. (2014). *Green Infrastructure for Landscape Planning: Integrating Human and Natural Systems*. New York: Routledge.

Beatley, T. (2000). *Green Urbanism: Learning from European Cities*. Washington DC: Island Press.

Beatley, T. (2010). *Biophilic Cities: Integrating Nature into Urban Design and Planning*. Washington DC: Island Press.

Benedict, M.A. and McMahon, E.T. (2006). *Green Infrastructure: Linking Landscapes and Communities. Urban Land* (Vol. June). Washington DC: Island Press.

Coutts, C. (2016). *Green Infrastructure and Public Health*. Abingdon: Routledge.

Dempsey, N., Smith, H. and Burton, M. (2014). *Place-Keeping: Open Space Management in Practice*. London: Routledge.

Fairhead, J. and Leach, M.(1996). *Misreading the African Landscape: Society and Ecology in a Forest-Savannah Mosaic*. Cambridge University Press, Cambridge.

Farina, A. (2006). *Principles and Methods in Landscape Ecology: Towards a Science of the Landscape*. London: Springer.

Fisher, D., Svendsen, E. and Connolly, J. (2015). *Urban Environmental Stewardship and Civic Engagement: How Planting Trees Strengthens the Roots of Democracy*. New York: Routledge.

Howard, E. (2009). *Garden Cities of To-Morrow* (Illustrated Edition). Gloucester: Dodo Press.

Jongman, R. and Pungetti, G. (Eds.) (2004). *Ecological Networks and Greenways: Concept, Design and Implementation* (R. Jongman and G. Pungetti, Eds.). Cambridge: Cambridge University Press.

Kaplan, R. and Kaplan, S. (1989). *The Experience of Nature: A Psychological Perspective*. New York: Cambridge University Press.

Keswick, M. and Hardie, A. (2003). *The Chinese Garden: History, Art and Architecture*. Cambridge: Harvard University Press.

Lachmund, J. (2013). *Greening Berlin: The Co-production of Science, Politics, and Urban Nature*. Cambridge: MIT Press.

Little, C. (1990). *Greenways for America*. Baltimore: John Hopkins University Press.

Louv, R. (2005). *Last Child in the Woods: Saving Our Children from Nature-Deficit Disorder*. Chapel Hill, NC: Algonquin Books.

Lynch, K. (1960). *The Image of the City* (Harvard-Mit Joint Center for Urban Studies). MIT Press.

McHarg, I.L. (1969). *Design with Nature* (Wiley Series in Sustainable Design) (25th Anniversary edn.). Hoboken: John Wiley and Sons.

Mell, I.C. (2015). 'Green infrastructure planning: policy and objectives'. In D. Sinnett, S. Burgess and N. Smith (Eds.), *Handbook on Green Infrastructure: Planning, Design and Implementation*, 105–23. Cheltenham: Edward Elgar Publishing Ltd.

Mell, I.C. (2016). *Global Green Infrastructure: Lessons for Successful Policy-making, Investment and Management*. Abingdon: Routledge.

Newman, A. (2015). *Landscape of Discontent: Urban Sustainability in Immigrant Paris*. Minneapolis: University of Minnesota Press.

Rouse, D.C. and Bunster-Ossa, I. (2013). *Green Infrastructure: A Landscape Approach*. Chicago: APA Planners Press.

Sinnett, D., Smith, N. and Burgess, S. (Eds.) (2015). *Handbook on Green Infrastructure: Planning, Design and Implementation*, Cheltenham: Edward Elgar Publishing Ltd.

Sturzaker, J. and Mell, I. C. (2016). *Green Belts: Past; Present; Future?* http://doi.org/10.4324/9781315718170.

Tate, A. (2015). *Great City Parks* (with Marcella Eaton) (2nd edn.). London: Routledge.

Tuan, Y-F. (1977) *Space and Place: The Perspective of Experience*. Minneapolis: University of Minnesota.

Policy papers and reports

Belfast City Council (2007). *Your future city: the Belfast agenda. A draft for consultation*. Belfast, UK.

CABE Space (2005). *Start with the park: creating sustainable urban green spaces in areas of housing growth and renewal*. London.

CABE Space (2009). *Making the invisible visible: the real value of park assets*. London.

Cambridgeshire Horizons (2011). *Cambridgeshire Green Infrastructure Strategy*. Cambridge: Cambridge Horizons.

Center for Neighborhood Technology (n.d.). *RainReady*. http://rainready.org/ (accessed 21 August 2018).

Central Park Conservancy (2016). *About us*. www.centralparknyc.org/about/about-cpc/ (accessed 21 August 2018).

Chicago Metropolitan Agency for Planning (2014). GOTO 2040 *Comprehensive Regional Plan*. Chicago.

Bibliography

Countryside Agency and Groundwork (2005). *The countryside in and around towns: a vision for connecting town and county in the pursuit of sustainable development.* Wetherby.

Davies, C., Macfarlane, R., McGloin, C. and Roe, M. (2006). *Green infrastructure planning guide.* Annfield Plain.

Department for the Environment, Food and Rural Affairs (2018). *25 Year Environment Plan.* London.

Department of Communities and Local Government (2012). *National Planning Policy Framework.* London.

England's Community Forests (2004). *Quality of place, quality of life.* Newcastle.

England's Community Forests and Forestry Commission (2012). *Benefits to Health and Wellbeing of Trees and Green Spaces.* Farnham. www.communityforest.org.uk/resources/case_study_health_and_wellbeing.pdf (accessed 21 August 2018).

European Commission (2012). *The multifunctionality of green infrastructure: in-depth report.* Science and Environment Policy, DG Environment News Alert Service. Brussels.

European Commission. (2015). *Towards an EU research and innovation policy agenda for Nature-Based Solutions and re-naturing cities. Final report of the Horizon 2020 Expert Group on "Nature-Based Solutions and Re-Naturing Cities".* Brussels.

Glasgow and Clyde Valley Green Network (n.d.). www.gcvgreennetwork.gov.uk (accessed 21 August 2018).

Grosvenor (2015). *'Living cities': our approach in practice.* London.

Landscape Institute (2009). *Green infrastructure: connected and multifunctional landscapes. Landscape Institute Position Statement.* London.

Landscape Institute (2013). *Green infrastructure: an integrated approach to land use. Landscape Institute Position Statement.* London.

Landscape Institute, and Town and Country Planning Association (2012). *Green Infrastructure Scoping Study WC080: Report undertaken for Department of Environment, Food and Rural Affairs.* London.

Liverpool City Council (2016). *Strategic green and open spaces review board: final report.* Liverpool.

London Organising Committee for the Olympic and Paralympic Games (2007). *Design Principles for the Olympic Park.* London.

Mayor of London (2016). *The London Plan: the spatial development strategy for London consolidated with alterations since 2011.* London.

The Mersey Forest (2015). *More for trees: the Mersey Forest Plan.* Risley Moss.

Ministry of National Development (2013). *A high quality living environment for all Singaporeans: land use plan to support future management.* Singapore.

Ministry of the Environment and Water Resources, MND Singapore and Center for Liveable Cities Singapore (2015). *Sustainable Singapore blueprint.* Singapore.

Natural England and Landuse Consultants (2009). *Green infrastructure guidance.* Peterborough.

New York City Environmental Protection. (2010). *NYC green infrastructure plan: a sustainable strategy for clean waterways.* New York.

Philadelphia Water Department (2011). *Green city, clean waters: the city of Philadelphia's program for combined sewer overflow control.* Philadelphia.

Ridgers, N.D. and Sayers, J. (2010). *Natural play in the forest: forest school evaluation (Families). A report produced for Natural England.* Liverpool.

Siemens, A.G. (2011). *Asian green city index: assessing the environmental performance of Asia's major cities.* Munich.

TEP (2005). *Advancing the delivery of green infrastructure: targeting issues in England's Northwest.* Warrington.

Town and Country Planning Association (2004). *Biodiversity by design: projects and publications*. London.

Town and Country Planning Association (2012). *Creating garden cities and suburbs today: policies, practices, partnerships and model approaches – A report of the garden cities and suburbs expert group*. London.

Treepedia website (n.d.) http://senseable.mit.edu/treepedia (accessed 21 August 2018).

Williamson, K.S. (2003). *Growing with green infrastructure*. Doylestown.

Index